P9-DBP-543

Date Due

Leonardo da Vinci

who followed the sinking star

A fascinating study of Leonardo da Vinci—master painter, sculptor and architect, scientist, engineer and inventor—an introduction to the most versatile genius of all time, with emphasis on his discoveries in science and his inventions in mechanics and engineering.

By the Same Author

ALBERT EINSTEIN

GALILEO: *First Observer of Marvelous Things*

Leonardo da Vinci

who followed the sinking star

by Elma Ehrlich Levinger

To follow knowledge like a sinking star
Beyond the utmost bound of human thought
Tennyson, *Ulysses*

*Illustrated with photographs and with
sketches from da Vinci's notebooks*

JULIAN MESSNER, INC.   NEW YORK

Published by Julian Messner, Inc.
8 West 40th Street, New York 18

*Published Simultaneously in Canada
By The Copp Clark Company, Ltd.*

Copyright 1954, by Elma Ehrlich Levinger
Printed in the United States of America

Library of Congress Catalog Card No. 54-10591

Third printing, 1962

ACKNOWLEDGMENT

The illustrations used in the book are from the collection of the Fine Arts Department of the International Business Machines Corporation

Contents

To Rose and Carl Newman
in loving gratitude for
an autumn friendship

Spring

in Florence

"Youth is wondrous, but how fleeting!"

—*Carnival Song of Lorenzo de' Medici*

Chapter 1

IT WAS springtime in Florence, a time of blossoming and of hope. From their fortress-strong palaces noblemen rode forth, brave in hunting array, with hooded falcons perched upon their wrists. Humble folks threw wide their windows, long sealed against the winter's rain and wind; swept the moldy rushes from their floors; and hastened to the market place to buy or at least to pretend to bargain for the goods temptingly displayed in a hundred stalls. Even the beggars, who huddled on the church steps to whine their woes, tried to arrange their musty rags in more seemly fashion as they raised hopeful faces to the first sunshine.

In Florence, in 1477, so boasted one of its citizens, every day brought the clamor and bustle of a fair. The raising of silkworms, the weaving of rare silks had transformed the quiet little town on the Arno into a teeming industrial center. A haughty Venetian merchant wandering through the market place confessed to his Florentine host that not even in Venice could be found lovelier or more richly garbed ladies. Or, he added, more fascinating shops to lure the passerby with carvings and jewels, silks of the most dazzling patterns and woolens of the finest weave.

"A city of princes," murmured the traveler. He did not seem to notice the half-naked child in a near-by gutter searching for his next meal among the rotten lettuce heads and artichokes. "Of princes like that young man approaching us, who bears himself like the son of a Medici banker."

The Florentine laughed. "He is neither prince nor banker's heir," he answered, "but an artist, the baseborn son of Piero da Vinci, the notary. Leonardo's father must be a very successful lawyer to judge by the son's embroidered linen and rose-colored silk cloak. Until his third marriage brought him lawful offspring, the old man considered Leonardo his heir. And it is likely he still makes him an allowance."

The gossip lowered his voice as Leonardo da Vinci drew nearer. Tall and slender, graceful of carriage, his golden hair gleaming beneath his black velvet beret, the youth recalled to the traveler a painting he had seen just that morning. During mass in the church of San Michele, the Venetian had wondered what mortal could be as beautiful as the pictured archangel; now the model in the flesh seemed to be walking through the bustling market place.

Between the stalls a peasant drove a shaggy gray donkey. The patient little creature staggered beneath the weight of two baskets of vegetables and fruits balanced across its back. When it stopped suddenly, the master tried to urge it on with kicks and blows.

"That will do, my friend!" Leonardo strode forward to lay a restraining hand on the peasant's shoulder. "Stop beating the poor creature and see why it refuses to go farther. I noticed it limped badly. Has it cut its foot?"

"And what business is that of yours?" The man was sullen but he feared to defy the handsome, richly dressed stranger.

Instead of answering, Leonardo knelt beside the quivering animal. He gentled it with murmured words and strokings from a hand as white and delicately formed as a woman's; then he lifted one of its tiny feet. With an angry exclamation the young man ripped off the shoe and thrust it under the master's nose. "See how badly it is twisted. It must have been torture for the beast to take a single step."

"How was I to know? Give the shoe to me. I'll go straight to the farrier, and . . ."

"Oh, no, I'll make sure your wretched animal will never wear it again."

Leonardo smiled and with a turn of his long slender fingers twisted the iron shoe as though it were his rose-colored silken cloak. Not only the peasant but the group of idlers who had gathered closer to listen to the argument gasped with astonishment.

Still smiling, Leonardo tossed the horseshoe into the gutter.

"But, sir," and now there was admiration as well as respect in the peasant's voice, "I am a poor man and can ill-afford a new shoe for my beast."

The youth, who had already turned away, swung back at the protest. His left hand fumbled in the embroidered pouch that hung at his waist; he drew out several coins. "Is this enough to buy a new shoe for the beast and a drink for the master?" he asked.

The man burst into loud thanks, but Leonardo turned abruptly and made his way through the gaping crowd. A moment later he paused in front of one of the stalls to study the wicker cages filled with birds of every size and species.

"He has not only the beauty but the strength of a pagan god," murmured the stranger from Venice. "Did my eyes deceive me or did he really twist that iron?"

His companion sneered. "Yes, I saw . . . and now I believe some of the tales I've heard of Master Leonardo. One would think those white hands were strong enough only to fret the lute or hold the paintbrush. For you must know he is esteemed as one of the sweetest musicians in all Florence; and since he was apprenticed to our great Verrocchio he has become the favorite pupil in his workshop. Well, I have heard it whispered more than once that young Leonardo has the Evil Power to thank for his skill and his beauty and his devil's strength."

He paused to make the sign of the cross to render harmless, at least for the time being, the one he had just mentioned. "Did you see how he used his left hand? As easily as I do my right! 'Tis said he draws and writes with it. Sinister! Men have been accused of witchcraft for less. When we are in a more private place, I will tell you. . . . But let our fine friend beware, or he'll find himself again behind the walls of the Bargello."

"Why was he imprisoned? It is hard to believe evil of him after looking upon his face," said the Venetian. He continued to gaze curiously at Leonardo, who was still standing before the booth of the bird sellers.

The Florentine hesitated; he seemed a little ashamed of his slanderous tongue but in a moment continued. "You already know of our *tamburini,* our boxes in which any citizen may deposit unsigned accusations?" The other nodded. "The names of Leonardo and several of his fellow students were mentioned in such an anonymous letter. They were charged with most unseemly conduct. Nothing was proved and all shortly regained their liberty." He laughed grimly. " 'Tis said that as soon as Leonardo was freed he devised a clever iron tool, a sort of jack with screws for drawing nails, which easily opens locks. Perhaps our inventor fears new scandals may arise and is trying to prepare himself against new imprisonment."

"But why does he buy two cages of birds?" asked the visitor from Venice, as Leonardo at last moved down the street with a bird cage hanging from each hand. "Surely he does not intend to cook all of them for his supper."

"Another of his whims! He is said to abhor the flesh of bird and beast and fish and seldom eats aught but fruits and vegetables."

"Then why . . . ?"

"You'll not believe this, I'm sure, but 'tis common gossip in Florence. He often buys birds—sometimes a huge hawk, again a cage of tiny larks—to set them free. Then he lies for hours on a hill beyond the city, watching their flight and noting down their movements in that little book he carries fastened to his girdle."

"But why . . . ?" began the Venetian again and was again interrupted.

"No doubt he uses birds in the devising of his cursed spells." For a second time the Florentine made the sign to ward off evil. "Do you think I am just repeating idle tales? My sister's son was one of the apprentices when Leonardo first came to Verrocchio's workshop. The boy has told me there were many godless drawings in Leonardo's notebooks with inscriptions no one could read. Poor lad! For weeks he limped from a beating Leonardo gave him, merely because my nephew wanted to amuse himself by hanging a cat. So you will agree that I have all my stories from one who knows Leonardo da Vinci well and knows the truth above him."

The Venetian merchant smiled but changed the subject.

Chapter 2

 EANWHILE Leonardo da Vinci, a wicker cage swinging from each hand, strode through the crowded market place. He appeared unconscious of the smiles, malicious or pitiful, that greeted his unusual purchase. Soon he reached one of the fifteen gates in the fort-crowned walls that encircled and protected Florence from her envious rival city-states.

For a moment Leonardo lingered to watch the throngs of travelers about to enter the city. Here at Florence the roads from north and east and west brought pilgrims from far-off places; before they journeyed on to Rome they exchanged their foreign currency at the tables (*banchi*) that lined the street. He seemed to study the strangers with an artist's sensitive appreciation of all that was new and arresting in their garb and manners. But his heart burned with a great pity for their helplessness.

A few of these pilgrims rode in coaches or astride noble horses; but the majority came afoot, their garments stained with the dust of the roads, their shoes in tatters, their faces hunger-pinched and weary. Leonardo knew the money-changers would show no mercy to Christ's poor; they would contrive to give the lowest possible exchange since they believed the civic authorities were conveniently deaf and blind.

Some of these businessmen, Leonardo always reminded himself wryly, became so rich they could afford to be patrons of the arts. They were willing to pay well for the paintings and sculptures that had transformed little Florence into the glory of the Renaissance. Yet sometimes he hated them all, from the magnificent beauty-loving Medicis who ruled the state down to the humblest money-changer who preyed upon the helpless pilgrims.

It was all a muddle, he thought, as in the bright spring sunshine he began to climb the white road that wound above the city. Business, as he saw it, was a sordid thing. His own father knew every trick of the lawyer's trade and turned many a shady bargain. But the money Piero da Vinci earned through his profession helped to pay for Leonardo's fine linen and his new rose-colored cloak; for wine, when it came his turn to pay the score at the tavern; yes, even for such nonsense, so his father would call it, as the purchase of twisted horseshoes and these imprisoned swallows.

Leonardo was successful for one who had so recently become a master painter, but his generosity even more than his love for gracious and luxurious living often left him with empty pockets. Although in his twenties he still turned to his father for support.

He angrily tossed his shining head and climbed higher. He was an artist, he told himself, and, by God's grace, maybe an inventor. Tomorrow or the day after or the day after that, with a light heart and a heavy purse he would confront his old father and tell him he no longer needed his grudging gifts!

Leonardo paused to look down on Florence, his lovely City of the Lilies, glittering and golden in the afternoon sunlight. Above the brightly hued roofs pointed many towers, round, squat, or slender. Proudly rising above them all gleamed the dome of the cathedral and the whiteness of the campanile, from which at that very moment the bells tolled the hour with their many brazen tongues.

Leonardo's climb had left him heated and a little tired. He threw himself upon the ground and closed his eyes. But a chirping from one of the cages he had just set down immediately roused him. He sat up and spoke to the swallows now huddled in a frightened heap in one corner.

"Are you weary of your prison, little brothers?" he asked. He smiled as he recalled a legend he had just discovered in his random and seemingly purposeless reading. The swallow, so declared an ancient naturalist, when she discovers that her fledglings have been caged brings them poison berries to eat. Leonardo had recorded the superstition in his notebook and added: "Better death than loss of liberty." Now he opened the door of the wicker prison and thrust in his hand for one of the birds. It pleased him that after a moment's struggle the little prisoner seemed to lose all fear and blinked at him with trustful eyes.

"Have patience, little friend," murmured Leonardo. "I shall not be long. Let me spread your wing—so. Quiet! I shall not harm you." He held the bird in a secure but painless grip; with his free left hand he opened his small notebook and quickly sketched the outspread wing.

"How does it differ from the lark's?" he puzzled. "Perhaps I shall find some difference if I study the last sketches I made of the arrangement of a lark's wing feathers. But I am sure the principles of flight will remain the same."

Having completed the drawing, Leonardo loosened his hold. For a moment the bird cuddled in the friendly palm which nested it; then it rose exultingly toward the silver gray branches that arched overhead. The four remaining swallows Leonardo released together; they rose and dipped above him. He watched their flight with passionate attention until the diminishing little bodies faded against the sky.

He turned a page and inscribed another note, writing, as he often did, from right to left. He had begun to employ this mirror-script years ago. Although they could be easily deciphered when held before a mirror, the notes could not be read if an unexpected visitor surprised Leonardo at his desk. Notes and drawings of the wings of birds and bats, observations on geology, the methods by which fish swim were not so likely to bring censure as some of Leonardo's

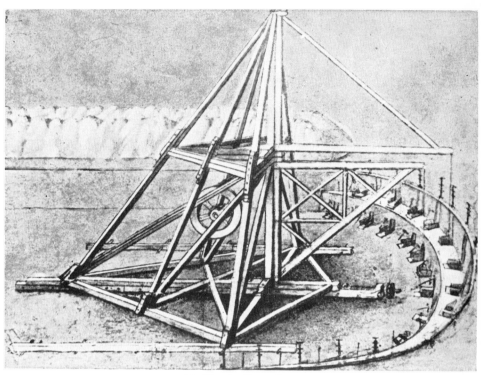

Machine for Excavations

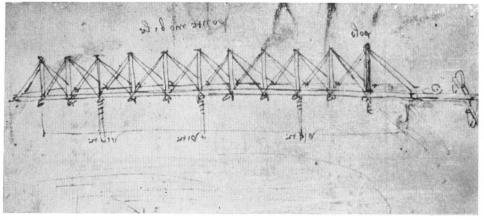

Military Bridge

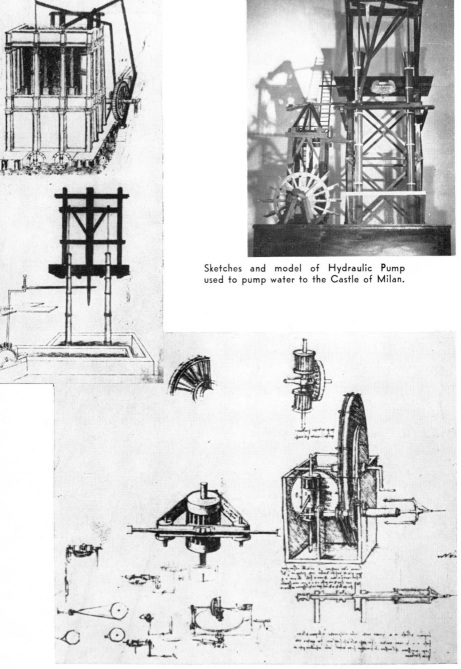

Sketches and model of Hydraulic Pump used to pump water to the Castle of Milan.

Flyer Spindle—Wound thread on a spool by revolving the spool, at the same time moving the guide back and forth.

Mona Lisa

Virgin of the Rocks

Studies of Equestrian Monument

Leonardo's Mirror Writing

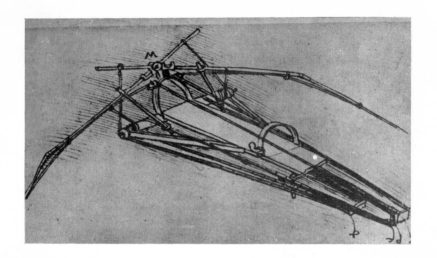

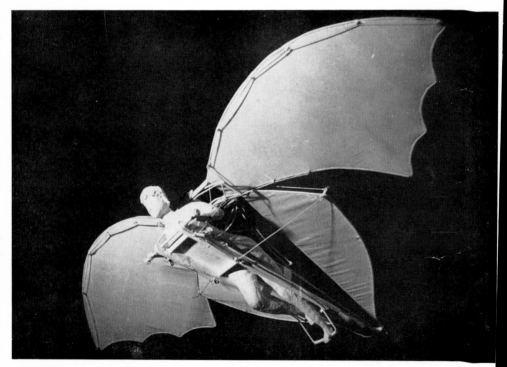

Flying Machine (Ornithopter)—Artist's sketch and a model of the invention. Lying prone in the frame, his feet in leather stirrups connected by pulleys to the wings, the flyer was to move his feet up and down to flap the wings. At the same time he was to operate the windlass with his arms and guide the machine.

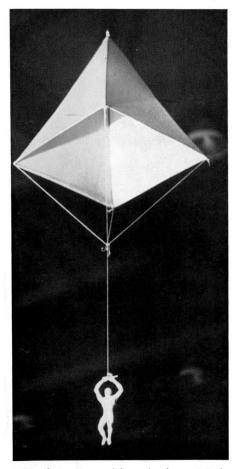

Parachute—A model and the original sketch. Pyramid-shaped "tent of linen" as Leonardo called it, believed to have been tried out successfully in his own day from a tower especially built for the purpose.

Circular Pulley
System

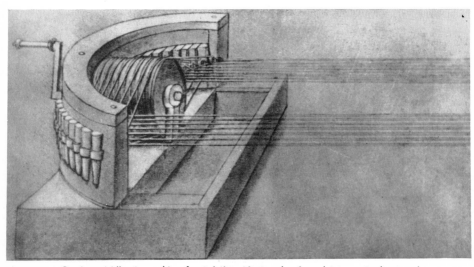

Catapult—Operated by turning a winch which drew back a flexible piece of wood fashioned like a bow. When suddenly released, the bow flew upward, striking a pivoting crossbar to which was attached a sling containing the missile to be hurled.

Cordage Mill—A machine for twisting 18 strands of cord into a single strand

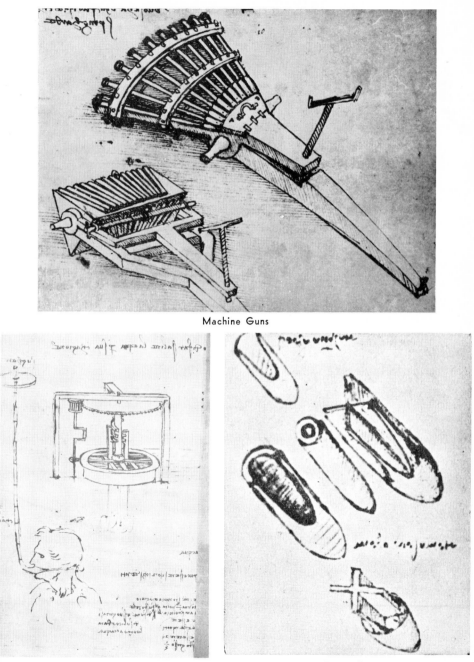

Machine Guns

Diver's Apparatus

Projectiles

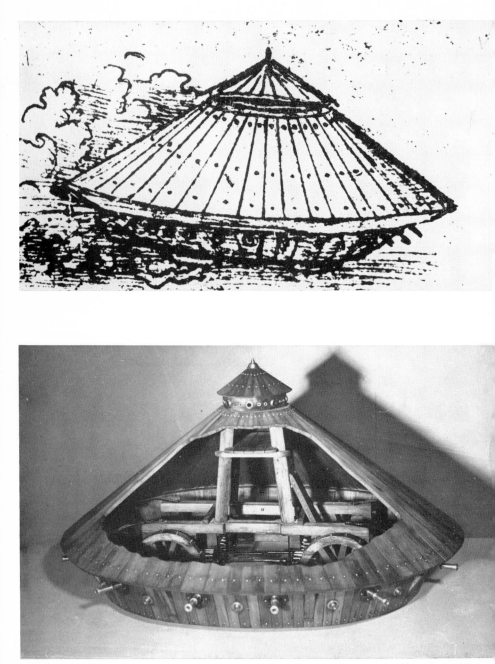

Military Tank—Artist's sketch and a model. Designed for breechloading cannon. Shaped to withstand impact of cannon balls.

criticisms of church and state. And he realized that his jottings concerning his vision of a day when men would move through the air like birds would only increase the scorn of his enemies who already regarded him as half-mad. He knew that he must guard his dream until the shining hour of his triumph.

Now he set down that birds which fly in spurts, like the swallow, rise to a height by beating their wings. Next he made a hasty note to remind himself to write down in full the results of his dissection of the jaw of a crocodile, which, happily for the investigator, had just died in the zoo of Lorenzo the Magnificent. Another note: Take out a bull's liver to make an anatomy. Swiftly he added the thought that had just seized him: Why is the fish in the water swifter than the bird in the air when it ought to be the contrary, seeing that water is heavier and thicker than the air and the fish is heavier and has smaller wings than the birds?

Leonardo reluctantly closed his notebook. Turning to the larger cage that confined the hawk, he released the captive and watched with narrowed eyes as it quickly soared out of sight.

Some day, he thought, I must study that proud fellow more closely—as well as the falcon and other birds of prey. Though they all seem so strong in their swift cruelty, they are weak beside the eagle. Even his wings would be far too puny to bear a man through the clouds. Yet the principle of flight must be the same! Once I grasp it and fashion wings for man, the Great Bird will no longer be a Grecian fable or a childish dream.

He restored his notebook to his girdle. Then, stretched at full length, his hands clasped behind his head, he stared through the leaves above him at the still unconquered sky. As he had so many times before, both in his daydreams and in the terrifying visitations of the night, Leonardo again seemed to see the Great Bird which had hovered above his sleep in a peasant's hut in Vinci.

Chapter 3

*L*EONARDO had carried away from Vinci two memories of his otherwise forgotten childhood, memories to be fitted, as time went on, like polished pebbles into the brilliantly enameled mosaic which became his life. Tiny shells forever imprisoned in the ancient rocks. . . . The bones of a huge fish. . . . These formed Leonardo's second memory of the village that was his birthplace.

The first memory was of the Great Bird, surely a vulture, frightfully large and very, very near, as it flapped its shrouding wings over the bed where the child Leonardo slept.

All through his life Caterina's son relived that dream. His rational manhood recognized it as such; it was only a dream of a terrible bird that paused in its hoverings to strike the boy's face again and yet again with its smothering tail. Little Leonardo awoke from his dream, screaming for his mother to drive away the enemy with wings.

The years like a rolling river swept away recollection of the words she had murmured to reassure him, the shape of her comforting hands. Soon he found it impossible to recreate the face which had bent over him; all faded but the smile, warm, yet remote and mysterious through its detached pity. But the growing boy never forgot how she had lifted him in her strong, reassuring arms and held him close while she sang a song of the countryside until he drifted off on a river of untroubled sleep.

It seems a pity that Leonardo who worshiped beauty so passionately, was destined never to place on canvas her patient smile, her bright hair. Caterina's was the loveliness so often found in peasant girls of the Latin races, a beauty at once shy and challenging, shadowed by the dignity which the harsh years harden to flinty strength. Although she was but a serving maid at an inn near Vinci, her proud carriage and low voice led young Piero to believe the rumor that she was of gentle blood.

But even in the madness of his first love, Piero knew that he could never marry a servant, a girl of unknown parentage. For generations his family had been highly respected in the little town of Vinci from which it derived its name. Here, several days' journey from Florence, the da Vincis had long served as notaries. They had spent their fees shrewdly on land purchases. Old Antonio, Piero's father, was proud of his lineage, of his comfortable estates. He had long desired a grandson to whom to leave his wealth and honorable name. But when he learned that Caterina, a serving maid at the inn, was soon to bear Piero's child, he refused to allow their marriage to be legalized.

Piero trembled before his father's threat of disinheritance. He did not trust himself even to bid farewell to Caterina; instead he journeyed to Florence and sought distraction in the details of drawing up a will for one of his father's clients. He returned home to learn that Antonio had provided Caterina with a dowry, modest but large enough to induce a herder of cattle on a nearby estate to marry her.

By the time Piero's son, whom the mother named Leonardo, was born, Antonio da Vinci had arranged another marriage. Children seldom dared to rebel against their parents' wishes in the Italy of 1452. Piero, at his father's bidding, married Albiera, a charming young woman of somewhat higher social standing than his own.

One, three, five years passed and still there was no grandson born in the great stone house that old Antonio had fondly hoped would shelter his son's sons and their children after them. He sighed whenever he thought of little Leonardo, son of a serving maid, who, the village gossips reported, had inherited not only Caterina's bright beauty but Piero's cleverness of brain and tongue.

Late one spring afternoon the frustrated grandfather went in secret to the hut of the herdsman who had married Caterina. She was sitting by the vine-covered door spinning, while the golden haired youngster sat nearby, watching with absorbed eyes a fligh of cranes against the sunset. At his mother's bidding he turned reluctantly to greet the well-dressed stranger.

"The birds fly . . . and fly . . . and never fall," he murmured.

He courteously answered Antonio's questions and with a gracious smile brought him a cup of cool water from the nearby well. Antonio was charmed by the handsome boy's manners and his ready speech. How could the child have learned them from a servant girl in a peasant's hut, he puzzled.

That night he told his aging wife, Mona Lucia, of his plans; she eagerly agreed to take Leonardo into their childless household.

"He is really our grandson," she said and her eyes grew tender with longing. "You know how much I have desired grandchildren. And if the gossip of our servants can be trusted, his foster father, who is a bitter, surly man, will be glad to be rid of Leonardo. But will you be able to persuade his unhappy mother to part with him?"

No one ever knew what words passed between Antonio da Vinci and the still girlish Caterina, while her husband snored in the chimney nook and her son slept on his pallet in a corner of the dimly lamplit room. But at the end Caterina bowed her head weeping, and Antonio, the notary, made a gesture to the manservant who waited beyond the threshold. Nor did she raise her eyes when, obedient to a nod from his master, the servant lifted the sleeping boy in his arms. So little Leonardo left his mother's home forever, to live in the great stone house Antonio had built to shelter his son's children and their children after them.

Like all young children the five-year-old boy marveled little at the sudden change in his fortunes. He missed his mother's caresses and at first cried when he was forbidden to run off and visit her. But his young stepmother Albiera was also tender and loving. It was as though she sought to find in Leonardo the son she had so vainly prayed for. Her husband agreed that until she bore him an heir it might be well to rear and educate little Leonardo as a da Vinci. The bachelor uncle Francesco made a great pet of the boy; Grandmother Lucia coddled and spoiled him, seeming to forget her strictness when her own children were growing up around her.

Grandfather Antonio also overindulged his only grandson. Some time earlier he had turned over the affairs of the estate to an overseer. But, still active in body and mind, he delighted in taking long walks, now more than ever since Leonardo proved a pleasant companion on such rambles.

Soon after setting out, they could look down on Vinci where the houses nestled in the shadow of the towered castle. On and up they climbed toward the never-reached heights of Monte Albano in all its glittering whiteness. Often the old man was forced to sink on a mossy stone to rest. But young Leonardo never seemed to tire. He would disappear in the underbrush to track down a rabbit or follow the call of a hidden bird; or he might run ahead along the twisted path to gather a flower or pick up a pebble to treasure in the corner cupboard in his room beneath the eaves.

It was from one of these walks in the shadow of Monte Albano that Leonardo carried away the second memory of his childhood. This was etched in even stronger colors than the earlier, oft-recurring picture of the Great Bird, for by this time he was nearing his tenth birthday.

Old Antonio had taken him for a day's pleasuring in the foothills. While the grandfather rested after their noonday meal of bread and cheese, figs and wine, the boy climbed higher than he had ever ventured before. There among the rocks he made an almost incredible discovery—several cockle and oyster shells and bits of seaweed, petrified in an eternal perfection as they rested more than a hundred miles distant from the sea waves which had bred them.

Leonardo filled his pockets with the fossils, then hastened down the path. The old man drowsed in the sleepy sunshine. The boy, inconsiderate for the first time, excitedly shook him into wakefulness.

"Grandfather, grandfather, see what I've found! Seashells. Seashells so far from the sea. What could have brought seashells to rest upon a mountain side?"

Antonio da Vinci for all his wisdom could not answer him.

Nor could Father Alberto, the gentle old priest who had taught him to read and write. "Shells so far from the sea?" He repeated the latest of his pupil's many questions. Surely Leonardo remembered the story of the Flood which God had sent to destroy sinners in the days of the righteous Noah. "My boy," he said, "if you would only concern yourself with what is really important. Your father is esteemed as a notary not only in Vinci but even in Florence. How can you expect to take his place when you grow up if you remain ignorant of Latin?"

The teacher added something about the necessity of beginning the study of Greek, recently revived among Italian scholars, after many centuries of neglect. But, who wanted to be a notary? Leonardo asked himself scornfully. Or a scholar with his nose glued to a Latin or Greek text? I'm going to climb even higher next time, he resolved, and maybe I'll find more strange and wonderful things.

Several years after Leonardo had found his first fossils he discovered a cave which impressed him so greatly that in manhood he described it not once but several times in his notebooks. The dark hollow among the rocks captured his imagination and appeared again and again in his pictures, beginning with the one he painted while still a boy in Vinci. Years later he described his adventure:

> . . . drawn on by my eager desire, anxious to behold the great abundance of the buried and strange forms created by artificer Nature, having wandered for some distance among the overhanging rocks, I came to the mouth of a huge cavern before which for a time I remained stupefied, not having been aware of its existance. . . . I was bending continually first one way and then another in order to see whether I could discern anything inside

though this was rendered impossible by the intense darkness within. And after remaining there for a time, suddenly there was awakened within me two emotions, fear and desire, fear of the dark threatening cavern, desire to see whether there might be any marvelous thing therein.

It is easy to consider this as an allegory, which designated in no uncertain terms what was to be the ruling passion of Leonardo's turbulent life. With the sensitivity of the artist he was often to know fear and doubtings; but his desire to discover what was hidden in the darkness never failed to conquer any other emotion. And on this day of his youthful questing his curiosity was at once satisfied and whetted. For amid the debris which cluttered the darkness Leonardo found the whitened bones of a strange monster. Surely, he puzzled, a fish—but how, when the sea is so far away?

Whenever his father's business called him to Florence the youth deserted his books to roam among the woods and hills. Sometimes he did not return until the long dusk of summer had deepened into darkness. He would tiptoe up to his own little kingdom under the eaves. Here by the light of a candle he would survey the day's spoils: the leaf from a tree he could not name, the still warm body of a field mouse he planned to dissect on the morrow.

The leaf withered into dust. A housemaid complained that when she tried to clean the young master's room she became ill from a terrible smell. Grandmother Lucia investigated and discovered the remains of the field mouse cached in the corner cupboard. Leonardo didn't mind her scolding. But why, he complained reasonably enough, had she thrown the corpse away before he secured what might have proved a very interesting skeleton!

That he might retain his treasures the youth began to make hasty sketches during his walks. Piero viewed his son's first artistic attempts with an indulgent eye. If Leonardo were his only heir, which now seemed more than likely, he would be expected in due time to become his father's successor in the family's long line of notaries. But Piero da Vinci knew that in Florence and Venice and Rome it was now considered fashionable for a man of independent means, yes, even a nobleman, to dabble in music or poetry or

painting. Leonardo must become a successful lawyer, but his love
for sketching and lute-playing need not interfere with his destined
profession.

One day Leonardo drew a picture of his young stepmother as
she bent over the embroidery with which she tried to fill her empty
days. She had grown so frail and white that the boy wondered
whether she, too, would fade like the flowers he tried to preserve
on his tablets. As he studied her pale face, shadowed by the heavy
hair, her smile reminded him of his own mother. He wondered
whether his grandfather had sent Caterina far away. Or whether,
as a pitiful serving maid had whispered to him long ago, she had
died shortly after their parting. Albiera did not live long and
Leonardo wept bitterly at her passing for in her death he seemed
to lose his mother a second time. He could scarcely bear to look
at his picture which was all that remained to remind the da Vinci
household of Albiera.

Hardly were the days of mourning decently over when Piero
brought home another wife to comfort him for his loss. This Florentine girl, only a few years older than her stepson, did her best at
first to win his friendship. But Leonardo felt she was a usurper who
had no right to reign in the place of his dearly loved Albiera.

To make matters worse, a malicious relative hinted that this
sturdy young woman would surely bear Piero heirs to rob Leonardo
of his expected inheritance. By this time the youth realized that he
had no legal right either to his father's name or the family property.
The grandparents, who had always befriended him, had become
indifferent and withdrawn in their senility. His sense of insecurity
mounted. Leonardo grew more and more resentful of his father
and of his uncertain future. In his new surliness he was actually
rude to one of his father's friends.

This old neighbor had often admired the portrait of Albiera,
which Grandmother Lucia had proudly hung above the great stone
fireplace. One day he brought a large round plaque of wood, the
bark still clinging to its edges.

"The tree, which was tall and stately in my grandfather's time,
was sending its roots under my well. And so I had to cut it down,"

he explained regretfully. "Ever since I first saw your likeness of Mona Albiera," he told Leonardo, "I wondered whether you couldn't paint me a fine picture to hang above my fireplace. Use this plaque that I may always have it to remind me of the old tree. I want something bright and gay. Roses? And if it pleases me I will pay you. . . ."

Leonardo, who had been idly turning the pages of his bulky sketchbook, seemed suddenly deaf. Scowling, he rose and turned toward the stairs that led to his bedroom. But his father, whom Leonardo still feared to disobey, halted him sharply.

"Before you leave to fetch your paints and brushes to begin work," said Piero who was ever an agile thinker, "tell our old friend you will do your best to please him without a promise of payment." He spoke pleasantly enough but his stern eyes challenged his son to contradict him.

As soon as the visitor left, Leonardo burst into a storm of angry protests. "Do you think I'm no better than that painter who passed through Vinci last month?" he cried. "He promised a flattering likeness of anyone who crossed his palm with silver! I cannot paint roses or anything else on order."

"Go to bed, Leonardo," urged the grandmother as she watched Piero's scowl deepen. "I am sure that after a good night's sleep you will be sensible and willing to obey your father."

Leonardo hastened to his own chamber. But he was too irritated and excited to sleep. Instead he sat up in bed and by the moonlight that streamed through the window again examined his book of sketches.

Suddenly he chuckled. The very thing! He had already been fascinated by the grotesque as well as the beautiful: the tortured trunk of an ancient olive tree; the blank face of the village idiot who sat near the well staring listlessly into the sunshine. Why paint meaningless roses? The young artist's fingers itched to fashion a new and astounding horror.

I shall paint our flower-loving friend a real monster, exulted Leonardo. It will have the scales of the snake, a bat's face with the eyes of a rat, perhaps the snout of a pig. Why not give this terrible creature the shining rainbow wings of a gigantic butterfly? This mixture should be as frightening as the fire-breathing dragon in the altarpiece I saw when father took me to Florence—the dragon that lies all bleeding and writhing beneath the saint's spear. No man can swear that he has seen a dragon, so how can an artist paint an exact likeness? Better to picture one, then, as a combination of ugly and frightening creatures.

For the next few days the young artist shut himself in his own room; he worried his grandmother by refusing to appear even for his meals.

"He'll come to the table soon enough when he gets hungry," snapped Piero da Vinci's second wife. "I wonder what mischief that left-handed devil's brat is up to now."

But Mona Lucia, fearing for her grandson's health, ordered a maid servant to bring him his dinner. Leonardo unbarred the door at her knock, absent-mindedly thanked the girl and took the tray. A sip of goat's milk, a few mouthfuls of bread, a nibble of fruit; then he took up his brush again.

The background for his monster, Leonardo decided, must be as fearsome as the creature itself. He recalled the incident of the cave. Fear of the unknown, the threatening blackness, the broken bones of some mighty creature sunk deep in the uneven floor had added to his terror.

Now, remembering that terror, he drew for a background the mouth of the cave with all its blackness and mystery streaked with jagged lightning. He smiled as he threw his brush aside and flexed his weary fingers. "I believe my picture will say what I intend it to say," he murmured.

Carelessly Leonardo informed his father that the commissioned panel was finished.

"Come and see it," he invited, and Piero with a rather patronizing smile followed the lad up the stairs. At the open door of Leonardo's room he hesitated, blinking uncertainly. For the young artist had partially covered the windows and so arranged the picture that a single ray of sunlight fell directly upon it.

Piero da Vinci looked straight into the glaring eyes of a monster escaped from a madman's dreams. From jaws and nostrils the horrid apparition seemed to breathe living fire. The flames rose and fell. The notary, although never an imaginative man, could have sworn that he heard the crackle of flame and smelled the stench of sulphur. From the cavern which might have been the very mouth of hell the beast looked ready to spring upon him. Piero instinctively retreated.

"Are you frightened, father?" asked Leonardo with a maddening smile. "That is just how I intend people to feel when they look upon my picture."

Piero, already himself again, returned smile for smile. "I must confess I was a little surprised," he answered. "But have you forgotten that our neighbor desired you to cover his plaque with roses?"

"I preferred my little dragon," said Leonardo. "I wonder," he added teasingly, "whether our neighbor will be as fright . . . I mean as surprised as you were when he sees it."

Piero da Vinci decided that before delivering the gift, it might be safer to consult with Leonardo's old teacher, Father Alberto. The priest after one glance hastily made the sign of the cross and suggested that the abomination be burned. But the notary was a thrifty man. On his next visit to Florence he hurried to an art shop and selected a round plaque, polished wood adorned with crimson roses. The neighbor later thanked Leonardo effusively for painting him "such beautiful flowers." But the youth was at that moment absorbed in a study of goldfinches swaying on a pine branch and did not trouble himself to listen. The floral painting had cost Piero nothing, for the art dealer had presented it to him with a flourish— after paying the gratified father ten ducats for Leonardo's monstrosity!

A few months later Piero da Vinci was outraged to learn from a Florentine friend that the generous art dealer had sold the "abomination" to Galeazzo, Duke of Milan for three hundred ducats. Piero had heard many stories of that unfortunate ruler's vices and eccentricities. He was sure the duke had really gone insane to pay such a ridiculous sum.

Yet, pondered the shrewd notary, he is not the only wealthy

madman in Italy. If I have been informed correctly, there are many others who will pay well for a daub like the one it took my Leonardo a dozen hours to paint. I'm afraid he will never be a successful lawyer. I have seen him shrink with distaste when I boasted of my bargainings. And he is far too independent to flatter and cajole clients. 'I preferred my little dragon,' he told me—and painted it. Well, let him continue to paint dragons and sell them for a silly price to dukes and princes.

"Tomorrow," Piero da Vinci told his sixteen-year-old son, sure that this time there would be no opposition to his will, "tomorrow I shall take you with me to Florence. I have a will to draw up for the noble . . . but I see you are not interested. Perhaps this will help to hold your attention: I shall try to arrange that you serve your apprenticeship with any artist who is mad enough to take you into his studio."

Chapter 4

*I*F THE master to whose studio the sixteen-year-old Leonardo came to serve his apprenticeship was mad, it was only with a frenzy for accomplishment in many fields. He called himself Verrocchio, after his teacher, a famous goldsmith. As his varied skills developed, it was easy to understand why he had chosen the patronymic meaning "true eye." For Andrea del Verrocchio seemed to excel in every craft and art he undertook.

He first won fame as a worker in metals. Then he became esteemed as architect and mechanic and musician, only to be later acclaimed as among the first of Florence's artists and sculptors.

His *bottega* was a shop and school combined, where his pupil-apprentices learned to work with wood and marble and metal; one day they studied perspective; the next they looked over the master's shoulder while he frowned over a witch's brew of paints.

"Alas, my sons," Verrocchio might cry despairingly, "though I have labored for a month I am still as far from producing the desired color of Saint Joseph's robes as when I began. Let us fling this mess away and begin all over again."

It was Leonardo's good fortune to be enrolled in the school of an artist and craftsman like Verrocchio. The fall of Constantinople sixteen years before, in 1453, had sent a number of Greek scholars to seek refuge in Italy. They brought the rebirth of art and learning to Europe, for they carried with them their precious manuscripts which had been neglected during the Middle Ages. Now Florentines read and pondered the teachings of Plato. There was a revival of interest in philosophy, an upsurge of healthy doubting and questioning and experimentation. The mind of man began to travel far from home just as during Leonardo's middle manhood seaborne adventurers followed Columbus and Vasco da Gama in search of new routes across the world.

Of all the apprentices in the *bottega*, from boys of twelve to youths ready to join the Artists Guild and qualify as Master Painters, Leonardo was soon Verrocchio's favorite pupil. No student labored with the zeal of the youth from Vinci over the soldering of the cross to the copper ball which was to crown the dome of Florence's cathedral; or so readily understood the method the master had recently devised of stiffening folds of cloth with clay that they might be more easily painted.

Verrocchio was quick to discover his new pupil's searching mind; to appreciate the ingenuity of his seemingly effeminate fingers, equally at home with paintbrush, with chisel, with lathe and grindstone. The day Leonardo devised a pick far more efficient than the tool his master had been using, Verrocchio invited the youth to share another cup of wine after the other apprentices had finished their supper and gone to their own quarters behind the studio. For an hour or more the two sat at the long table talking of many things.

"I am well satisfied with you, my son," said Verrocchio. "A restless brain, a true eye, a clever hand! But it is a sad pity you brought such a scanty amount of book knowledge from your father's house. For example, what do you know of the Latin classics, or of Greek?"

Leonardo flushed with shame. "Nothing. But I have already started to study Latin, and the Greek writers I will read in translation. I am sure in their works I shall find the answers to many of the questions which trouble me."

"And mathematics? And mechanics?" Again Leonardo flushed

shamedly and shook his head. "I will read. I will learn," he
promised.

"Remember," counseled Verrocchio, pushing back his wine cup
and rising from the table, "remember that an artist must know many
things besides painting. Today it is the artist not the mathematician
who most zealously studies the laws of dimension. Some of us have
discovered that no piling on of draperies will conceal our ignorance
of the structure of the human body. What do physicians, those
pompous dispensers of pills and potions, know of the machinery
beneath the surface? But a few of us artists have become interested
in anatomy. You see, my son, if you aim to become a real painter
you have a great deal to learn."

The master turned toward the door of his own sleeping apartment
but Leonardo detained him.

"I have heard you say, sir, that behind all the arts and sciences
lie the laws of mathematics, especially geometry! I cannot afford to
buy books and instruments. But if you will lend me your Euclid I
shall guard it carefully."

Andrea del Verrocchio nodded, well pleased.

Now Leonardo began the studies and investigations that were to
continue through his long and crowded life. He spent hours over
the borrowed Euclid. He soon learned to love mathematics for its
exactness which helped to give him a feeling of security in an uncertain world.

He read much philosophy in these days, studied physics, and
attended scientific lectures. The youth with his genius for making
worthy friends was fortunate enough to win the interest of the re-
nowned Toscanelli, physician and mathematician. Toscanelli spread
before Leonardo the maps on which he had charted a westward
route to India, maps which were later to aid and encourage a still-
unknown Genoese sailor, one Christopher Columbus.

They talked long and earnestly together, the aging scientist and
the young art student, his eyes aflame with dreams. Toscanelli tried
to answer Leonardo's questions—of strange lands, dimly guessed
beyond the dark, tumbling seas; of the uncounted ages which had
left behind them the shattered skeleton in the cave near Vinci and

the strange shells upon the mountain slope. They talked also of the stars; Toscanelli lamented that astronomers were so poor in instruments which they needed to chart the bewildering heavens.

"Perhaps," Leonardo cried in his youthful confidence, "I shall invent . . ."

In those apprentice days, he did invent, along with tools for use in Verrocchio's workshop, certain instruments to measure time; one a water clock, the other to be operated by compressed air. Many of the drawings over which he labored long after the other youths had left their worktables and easels illustrated technical problems. His study of the Arno valley seemed at first glance rather the work of an architect than an artist.

Yet he progressed so rapidly in his painting that he easily took his place among the first of Verrocchio's students. It was the custom among the Italian studios that when the master received a commission for a painting, the most talented apprentice painters were permitted to fill in the background with minor figures. During his first years with Verrocchio, so ran the legend, Leonardo was chosen to paint a kneeling angel for the master's "Baptism of Christ." When Verrocchio looked upon his pupil's work, it is said, he threw down his brush and exclaimed: "I who have labored for so many years have been surpassed by this stripling. I will never paint again."

This seems an unlikely story since Verrocchio continued to paint. Perhaps the fiction first gained credence when Verrocchio, at the height of his fame as painter, began to direct all of his genius toward sculpture which was to add so largely to his reputation. But if the master were really irritated by the superiority of his pupil he seems to have been able to conceal his envy most successfully. He continued to regard Leonardo as his own son; when the apprentice days were over Verrocchio accepted him as a member of his own overcrowded household.

Chapter 5

*A*LTHOUGH he loved to express himself with brush and pencil, Leonardo might have grown restless in Verrocchio's studio had he been obliged to confine himself only to painting. But here he found great joy in working with every type of material: iron, silver, clay, and wood.

Leonardo would roam through Florence, pausing to transfer to his notebook every face that caught his fancy—a laughing girl with windblown hair; a serene mother, seated on her doorstep as she nursed her babe, never dreaming that she served as the first model of the earliest of Leonardo's madonnas. Or for a whole afternoon he would follow a bald, wrinkled man, studying the grotesque features until he had memorized every line and felt ready to draw the ancient's face from memory.

The next morning he would design a fantastic drinking cup for one of Verrocchio's lordly patrons; or the youth from Vinci would be called to decorate a wedding chest with pictures of the nuptials of the highborn pair against a background of doves and wreathed roses.

Sometimes every other project would be pushed aside. Then

every worker in the studio, from the master to the youngest of his apprentices, toiled feverishly to finish banners and helmets and shields tardily ordered for some Medici festival. The Florentines loved public spectacles and pageants; their Medici rulers, knowing well the value of a contented populace, delighted in satisfying their appetite. No wonder Leonardo came to believe that every saint in the calendar was honored by a splendid festival.

At the end of the Lenten season the dark-robed worshipers followed the image of the thorn-crowned Christ as it was borne down the saddened streets. As the faithful lamented and sobbed forth their sins, Leonardo looked across their bowed heads toward the spring-flushed hills and recalled the women who long ago wailed in chorus for Thamuz, slain in his youthful beauty. Or at Easter he would curiously watch the crowds who fought to see the sacred fire struck from stones brought from the Holy Sepulcher, and wonder at their excitement.

Midsummer awoke ancestral memories of heathen sacrifices in gratitude for golden grain and ripened fruit. Many ancient rites had been adapted and made acceptable by the Church; in this season the Florentines honored the city's patron saint, John the Baptist. The torches and the candles of the celebrants transformed the darkest church into a temple of the life-giving sun. There were incense and music, mounted processions of splendidly clothed knights and their ladies. When the glowing sun had disappeared behind the hills, huge bonfires blazed as though the citizenry of Florence still defied the powers of darkness and tried to prolong for a little while longer the burning brightness of Midsummer's Day.

Of all the festivals Leonardo da Vinci loved best the rites of May when the lightfooted dancers gathered before the house of the most openhanded and splendid of the Medicis, Lorenzo the Magnificent. They brought with them garlands of flowers still sparkling with the morning dew and sang the songs he wrote for them out of his hopeful youth and joy.

Leonardo, a lover of lyre and song, joined in their singing. Often Lorenzo sang also as he mingled with the dancers. He was several years older than Leonardo but when he threw his cares aside, the

head of the greatest banking house in the world and the ruler of
Florence and all Tuscany, romped like a merry schoolboy. Once in
the midst of the celebration, Leonardo wondered to see the poet's
eyes darken as though with pain.

Was it likely, thought Leonardo, that the prince believed that
even his triumphant youth would desert him on the morrow? No,
the artist decided, for when a man is young and it is spring in
Florence, how can he believe that the winter of old age will ever end
his happiness.

Leonardo soon forgot many of the songs Lorenzo composed, songs
for those who sang as they pressed the oil from the olives; songs
for the pastry cooks and the makers of gold thread; sacred poems
and verses not so sacred for the solace of young wives bound to old
husbands. But he never forgot Lorenzo's song for May Day, even
after Florence had become a lovely faded tapestry of what had been
his youth.

At these festivals, bright with youth and warm with springtime,
Leonardo's most constant companion was Atalante Miglioretti. They
were alike in many ways. Like Leonardo, he was distinguished for
his beauty even in Florence, a city of handsome youths and lovely
maidens. Atalante was a talented luteplayer and singer and a skilled
craftsman.

The two worked together on a shield and banner to be carried
in the tournament devised by Lorenzo the Magnificent. A plague
had shocked and saddened the folk of Florence; the latest of a
succession of wars between several of the Italian city-states had
brought suffering and death. The wily tyrant realized that it would
be well worth the thousands of gold florins the spectacle would cost
him if his uneasy subjects were amused and again lulled into
security.

Now Leonardo and his friend, arms entwined, stood in the
shadows of Santa Croce to watch the passing show. Leonardo
wondered idly how it would seem to be the son of a princely house,
to associate with these proud young lords who rode by. It would
be rather exciting, at least for a while, he thought, to sleep on a
bed of down in a noble chamber; to feast daily on dainties that

liveried servants offered on silver platters; to own and ride one of these high-bred steeds. With their coats groomed to a silken sheen, their waving manes and polished hoofs, the splendid animals seemed to be as gently bred, as carefully served, as their pampered owners.

If one is not lucky enough to be born a lord, mused Leonardo, he might be almost as fortunate to be my lord's favorite horse!

The multitude shouted a welcome as Lorenzo de' Medici rode by. On his red and white banner Verrocchio himself had painted the portrait of Lorenzo's loved lady, Lucrezia; on the Medici's escutcheon gold lilies bloomed on a blue field. The report passed from one awed spectator to another that the pearl in Lorenzo's cap cost the dizzy sum of five hundred ducats, the diamond that sparkled on his shield another two thousand. The wretches who had known the horrors of the plague, the cruel uncertainties of war, forgot their fears and sunned themselves in such magnificence.

But the glory of Lorenzo de' Medici was overshadowed by the gallant bearing of his younger brother, Giuliano, resplendent in silver trappings and a cap with feathers of woven gold, fastened with rubies of astounding size. It was this same Giuliano de' Medici who a few years later brought joy to every Florentine heart with the tournament he devised for the greater glory of his far-famed lady, Simonetta Vespucci.

Although Giuliano paid her this public honor and was her devoted knight, it was believed that he followed the Platonic cult of many lovers of that day and worshiped his beloved from a respectful distance. At least no one had ever heard the slightest complaint from her husband, cousin to the Florentine navigator, Amerigo Vespucci.

The lady in her frail loveliness had been painted by the greatest artists in Florence. Now Leonardo wished he might also paint her, a saint in a brocaded gown, as with modestly downcast eyes she swayed forward to place the victor's crown on Giuliano's bent head. It was easy to believe the report, thought Leonardo da Vinci, that no woman was ever jealous of the lady's beauty although so many men loved her to distraction. Ah, if he could only paint the pair of lovers as they stood there, capturing upon his canvas in unfading colors the touching loveliness of their youth!

Their cloudless, carefree lives seemed to him to be a personification of spring in Florence, so brief, yet so happy that it always brought sadness to the soul. Leonardo's eyes filled with tears although he could not read the future any clearer than the shifty-eyed fortune teller who jostled him for a better view. For the future was veiled alike to both astrologer and artist. Who could foresee that in twelve short months Simonetta, whose pathetic beauty Botticelli made immortal in his shell-borne Venus, would sicken of consumption and die? Or that in the year following his beloved lady's death Giuliano in all his youthful pride and gallantry would fall beneath an assassin's dagger?

Chapter 6

THE years Leonardo spent in Verrocchio's studio, from his six-teenth birthday through his middle-twenties, grew more and more productive. Of the pictures he painted in Florence too few survive; some are difficult to identify as his work, others remained un-finished. Many of his earlier works disappeared altogether, like the design for a tapestry for the king of Portugal, which has been described as a realistic and novel study of Adam and Eve in the Garden of Eden.

But in his ever bulkier notebooks he preserved endless sketches, the face of his dear friend, Miglioretti; a crone, withered and tooth-less; the head of a young girl bowed beneath the twisted, shell-like coils of her heavy hair. In many of these preliminary sketches could be seen the artist's increased striving for perfection. In prep-aration for his "Madonna with the Cat" he made study after study of the animal he loved so dearly—crouching, stiffly erect, relaxed in sleep. His pen drawings showed evidence of the mathematician guiding the artist's hand; the first sketches in the form of a high-pointed triangle; a later sketch showing the mother's arms forming a circle to hold her child; the last, a rectangle to frame the two figures.

Mingled with these art studies were drawings of many ingenious devices the majority of which Leonardo never finished. For not even his clever fingers could keep up with his lightning-swift brain. When he strolled over the countryside and paused to rest beside a millstream he was sure to jot down a new and better method for grinding wheat. If he waited for his supper at an inn he observed on what an inefficient spit the roast turned before the open fire. Out would come his notebook that he might set down the first draft of a self-turning spit which would leave the overburdened servant, who watched the meat, free to wait on the impatient guests.

None of his inventions put a single ducat into Leonardo's purse in his Florentine days. But as soon as his apprenticeship was over he expected to earn his living as a master painter. At the age of twenty-six he was permitted to join the Artists Guild and burn a candle to the painters' patron, Saint Luke. For in Europe in the year 1478 all craftsmen—and painters were classed among them—belonged to their own particular guild or union.

The pupils of Verrocchio, after serving their apprenticeship, were no longer expected to live together under his watchful eye. But because of his love for Leonardo the master accepted him as a member of his own household. This was fortunate. The master painter might now accept commissions and support himself by the sale of his pictures instead of assisting Verrocchio. But a beginner's earnings were scanty and uncertain.

Leonardo could not expect to live with his father. Although Piero da Vinci now lived in a fine residence in Florence he did not offer to set apart one of its many bedchambers for his first-born son. The notary had been pleased over Verrocchio's praises of his favorite pupil and the father's pride had prompted him to be indulgent whenever the young man asked for funds to support him in his extravagant mode of living. But there was an ever-increasing coldness between the two.

The grandparents, who might have urged reconciliation between father and son, were dead. Piero da Vinci no longer considered his oldest son his heir. On the death of his second wife, the aging but undiscouraged widower had promptly remarried. Margherita, the new stepmother, not only brought her bridegroom a large dowry, but in rapid succession rejoiced his heart with two sturdy boy babies, Antonio and Giuliano.

Piero had been greatly vexed by his first-born's early brush with the law, although Leonardo had been declared guiltless. His wife, eager that the former favorite should be displaced by her own children, constantly filled her husband's ears with rumors of Leonardo's daring (she called them impious) opinions. Whenever Leonardo, who never knew the value of a florin, ran into debt and appealed to his father, Margherita complained that the doting old father was robbing his infant children of their rights. Leonardo hated wrangling, especially over money matters; he decided he must fend for himself.

He had never allowed his painting to deflect him from his scientific interests. Shortly after coming to Florence he had started to ponder over engineering problems. Would it be possible, he asked himself, to turn the Arno into a navigable stream flowing from Florence to Pisa with its fine harbor? Since windpower was too uncertain, men turned more and more to running water, the only physical force that could be tamed to labor for their benefit. He began to design mills which would better utilize such power and to study other hydraulic problems. Even while he devised his homely mechanism for turning meat before a fire, Leonardo dreamed of great wings with which man might soar birdlike above the earth.

War came again to Florence. Now instead of sketches of flowers and madonnas Leonardo drew in his notebooks plans for instruments that might aid in the defense of the city. It is hard to understand how the gentle soul who in these same notebooks wrote with pity of the beaten donkey and the slaughtered lamb could coolly contemplate the manufacture of weapons with which to butcher his fellow man. He does not appear to have been inspired by patriotism, for Leonardo never seemed to have felt the slightest affection for his native Tuscany and changed his allegiance from one ruler to another as lightly as he changed from his rose-colored silk coat to one of purple velvet.

He had heard that the movements of artillery units were hampered because of the difficulty of handling heavy cannon. Why not produce lighter guns which could be carried on a less ponderous guncarriage? He designed a weapon that did not recoil when fired; also a many-barreled type of machine gun mounted on a base, geared to give it multiple action. Later he planned a huge machine much like a windmill, which could be turned to prevent the scaling ladders of the enemy from being set up against the walls of a besieged city.

These projects brought the inventor nothing but disappointment. Although many of Leonardo's suggestions were later utilized in warfare, his ideas were ignored by the military experts of Florence. If the war had lasted longer, one or another of Leonardo's daringly new ideas might have won the approval of the Medici generals. But the king of Naples, won over by Lorenzo the Magnificent's diplomacy, far more potent than his army, agreed to sign a peace treaty.

About this time Piero da Vinci, in spite of the coolness that had grown up between them, came to his son's aid. Leonardo might annoy his father with his extravagant habits and unconventional opinions, but the older man never forgot the praises Verrocchio had showered upon his most promising pupil. He did his best to secure for his improvident son a commission that would pay him a respectable fee. He spoke eloquently of Leonardo's talents to his clients, the monks of San Donato, and did not forget to quote all the flattering prophecies of the great Verrocchio. Piero was a good pleader; in 1480 he brought Leonardo a contract to paint an altarpiece for San Donato.

It was taken for granted by both patrons and artist that this work must illustrate a scriptural story. Printed books were still a rarity; reading was an accomplishment enjoyed only by scholars and priests. But none of the common folk, no matter how ignorant, could miss the meaning of what he saw painted in bold colors on the walls of church and convent and monastery. The faces of

Hebrew king and patriarch, the soldiers who gambled at the foot of the cross, the Holy Family were all as familiar to the worshipers as their own neighbors.

At first Leonard worked feverishly on the popular subject of the "Adoration of the Shepherds." For some reason his interest lessened and he turned to another phase of The Nativity, the arrival of the Magi at Bethlehem. He sketched study after study of the figures he planned to group about the Madonna and her newborn child: feeble old men, a youth lost in wonder. He worked with great intensity on the horses he meant to show in the background, splendid prancing animals which had borne their kingly riders to the light-filled stable.

The monks grew impatient, but Leonardo in his passion for perfection refused to be hurried. At last the preliminary studies were completed; now he was able to visualize the scene as he meant to paint it and the message it should carry to all who looked upon his altarpiece. Leonard hoped that every spectator would share the emotions of his pictured characters, who gazed on the miracle, as he put it, "with wonder in their faces . . . giving various expressions to their admiration as though the Host were being shown to them."

When Leonardo finally transferred his drawing, still unfinished, to the wall of San Donato, the monks and every visitor to the convent seemed to experience the reverence which Leonardo had striven so hard to inspire. Like his dramatic study of Saint Jerome, which he began during this period, the "Adoration of the Magi" also remained unfinished. For, as it happened again and again, Leonardo suddenly lost interest in his latest work.

Why should he continue to paint, he asked himself bitterly, when he was personally slighted and his work went unappreciated?

Leonardo felt the humiliation deeply when he was not included in an invitation to decorate the papal chapel that was to honor forever the name of Pope Sixtus IV. It seemed to him that every other Florentine artist of any pretensions had been summoned to Rome. To be sure Botticelli, the tanner's son, was his senior; although Leonardo might feel the lack of robustness in the older man's work, he was forced to acknowledge the mystic spell of his "Birth of Venus," his madonnas, and the ever radiant "Spring."

But not only had older artists received the honor of a call to Rome. What about Leonardo's former fellow-student, Perugino? Leonardo had admired the youth's devotion to his art; he had endured bitter privations while painfully accumulating the fees for his training. The two boys had become Verrocchio's favorite pupils. While Leonardo groped and meditated and dreamed, Perugino, untroubled by doubts and yearnings, had doggedly fought his way to financial security. He managed to secure commission after commission; he never agonized over the correct and conventional saints whom he drew, and never failed to deliver exactly when promised. He never refused an order; his one thought seemed to be to accumulate enough gold to keep forever from his door the poverty that had so long plagued him.

Yet this plodder with the soul of a peasant and the imagination of an ox, thought Leonardo bitterly, is called to Rome. And Ghirlandaio and Rosselli and others of more or less note are also summoned to Rome. Only a few second-class painters and I will remain neglected in Florence. I wonder that brat, Michelangelo, has not been honored with a commission for the Sistine Chapel. Perhaps he has, but Lorenzo the Magnificent refuses to allow his pet out of his sight!

Although the older artist would have laughed scornfully at the idea, Michelangelo Buonarroti, the boy prodigy of Florence, was at this time another thorn to prick Leonardo's professional pride. Shortly after his graduation from Ghirlandaio's studio, the youth had easily won what Leonardo had never been able to achieve, the patronage of the all-powerful head of the Medici family.

Leonardo's lips curled with scorn when he first heard the story of the earliest meeting between Lorenzo de' Medici and his protégé. Lorenzo, who had established an academy for young artists, had discovered the boy sculptor completing his work on the head of an aged faun.

"You have given him many wrinkles, so he must be very old,"

commented Lorenzo. "But you seem to have forgotten that the aged seldom have a set of perfect teeth."

The youth, so ran the tale, seized his chisel, and, after knocking out several teeth, indented the jaw in such a manner that the faun's face took on the sunken, toothless look of extreme old age. Lorenzo was so delighted with the boy's response to his criticism that he actually invited Michelangelo to become a member of his household, where he ate at his patron's table and studied under the tutors Lorenzo had provided for his own sons.

Leonardo knew that Lorenzo was a lover of classical art, which he collected for his palace and gardens and the museum he had established. Although he was also interested in contemporary sculptors and painters and often purchased their works, up to this time the Florentine tyrant had not bought a single picture from Leonardo or given him a single commission.

It was fortunate for Leonardo that when he grew thoroughly discouraged over his prospects in Florence, his old master Verrocchio was able to come to his rescue. The painter and craftsman had lately reaped sensational fame as a sculptor; his bronze "David" had won the honor of being exhibited in the Palazzo Vecchio; his statue of Saint Thomas had become one of the art treasures of Florence; the "Boy and the Dolphin" charmed all who entered the fairyland gardens of Lorenzo the Magnificent.

Curiously enough, Verrocchio seems to have introduced his former pupil to Lorenzo de' Medici not as artist but as a musician. A lover of all the arts, the poet-prince admired Leonardo's verses and his pleasing voice. But he admired most the silver lute on which Leonardo played.

The singer's own invention, the instrument was shaped to represent a horse's head with the animal's teeth serving as frets to indicate the tones. Lorenzo was quick to admire both the curious design and the lute's rich timbre.

It happened that at this particular time Lorenzo was eager to win the allegiance of Ludovico Sforza, the virtual ruler of Milan. Duke Ludovico was reputed to be a great lover both of music and of princely toys. The silver lute would be an appreciated gift, and if Leonardo da Vinci chose to bear it himself . . .

Leonardo had just become interested in planning an instrument which would weigh the air and be useful in determining a change in the weather. But he was willing to lay his unfinished work aside, and eagerly accepted the Medici's suggestion.

For he had heard rumors that Duke Ludovico planned to erect a colossal equestrian statue in honor of his famous father, Francesco Sforza. The bits of sculpture Leonardo had worked on during his apprentice days had added nothing to his reputation, but he felt he had acquired the necessary skill and experience in Verrocchio's *bottega*. He knew that Verrocchio's recommendation would count heavily in his favor since the master's heroic presentation of the "Colleoni" had recently become the admiration of all Italy.

Leonardo suddenly turned opportunist. Even if he did not receive the commission for the statue, at least he might persuade the duke to consider some of his wartime sketches. Florence no longer seemed in need of a military engineer; but the ruler of Milan, ever in the shadow of an enemy's attack, might turn a favorable eye on Leonardo's many neglected projects.

Atalante Miglioretti, the musician, accompanied Leonardo to the duke's court. The notary's son carried with him a letter of recommendation from Lorenzo de' Medici and the curiously shaped silver lute. His dear friend bore a sheaf of sketches and a number of unfinished pictures. Leonardo was now thirty years old. He knew the springtime of his life was ended. He felt that he had accomplished little in Florence. But his heart was warm with hope as he journeyed from the city—where so many of his youthful dreams lay buried—to begin a new life in Milan.

Summer

in Milan

"The natural desire of good men is knowledge"
—*from the notebooks of Leonardo da Vinci*

Chapter 7

*A*T FIRST it seemed to Leonardo da Vinci that all his high hopes would blossom and bear fruit in Milan.

The fifteen-year-old Duke Gian Galeazzo was the acknowledged ruler over the city-state of Milan. But his uncle, Ludovico Sforza, since the death of his elder brother, had assumed one prerogative after another and now waited impatiently to usurp full authority. So it was to the wily Il Moro, as Ludovico was called because of his Moorlike complexion, that Leonardo brought the gift of the silver lute.

Il Moro accepted the instrument graciously. He was eager to rival Lorenzo de' Medici as a patron of the arts; he discussed with Leonardo music and poetry and the superiority of the language of Tuscany over every other Italian dialect. Yes, he answered Leonardo's carefully phrased suggestion, it was indeed true that he was interested in the erection of a colossal bronze monument in honor of his heroic father. His deeply lamented brother, father of the reigning young duke, had cherished such a project years ago. But first . . .

Leonardo already knew that Milan was threatened by its enemy

51

Venice, strong alike in trade and war. He felt that Il Moro, for all his pretensions, was not at the moment interested in him as a Florentine artist. This was not the time, he decided, to discuss plans for the statue which Leonardo dreamed might rival Verrocchio's equestrian masterpiece. And it would surely be a waste of time to spread before the duke certain unfinished canvases and beg for a commission to complete them.

"If my new master's greatest interest lies in other projects," Leonardo told his friend, Atalante Miglioretti, "I must make such projects my chief concern and seek to interest him further."

That night long after his companion had fallen asleep Leonardo turned the pages of the notebooks he had brought with him from Florence. Here was an idea, he decided, that might appeal to Duke Ludovico. Perhaps if he elaborated the design of this hastily sketched weapon. . . . Dawn crept through the chamber windows and birds began to chirp beneath the eaves, but Leonardo still bent doggedly over his bulky memoranda.

In the prospectus Leonardo prepared for the duke he gave the greatest prominence to what he felt would command the attention of the head of a state constantly threatened by war. He wrote that he had worked out a method to construct bridges, light enough to be carried easily, yet strong enough to support armed troops; such bridges might be thrown across a stream by warriors pursuing or fleeing from an enemy. He described mortars that not only would cast deadly stones but would cause terror and confusion with their smoke. He boasted of being able to build covered chariots so insulated that they would survive any attack and hew a path for the infantry that might safely follow them. Also, he was confident that he knew how to empty the water from the moats that protected a besieged fortress; he sketched his proposed device for climbing a citadel's walls undetected. Among other death-dealing tools, Leonardo offered the design of a projectile filled with gunpowder and balls which he labeled "the most lethal machine that exists."

Leonardo presented one deadly object after another as lightly as in other days he had drawn an angel's head or an innocent flower. Was he so charmed by the intricacy of these devices that he gave no thought to what horrible ends they might some day be used? Or were the armored tank and the explosive bomb he drew without compunction no more real to him than the huge bird which he dreamed would carry him above the peaceful mountain snows?

After he had listed his many instruments of destruction, taking care to omit any detail which might betray his secrets to the duke's military staff, Leonardo suddenly decided to mention his other talents.

"In time of peace," he wrote, "I believe I can give perfect satisfaction . . . in architecture and the composition of buildings, public and private; and in guiding water from one place to another."

Although the carving and sculpture he had created in Verrocchio's workshop had added little to his artistic reputation, Leonardo went on to state with unusual confidence:

"Item. I can carry out sculpture in marble, bronze or clay, and also I can do in painting whatever may be done, as well as any other, be he who he may."

Then in a final attempt to remind the duke of the hope for the commission that had lured the artist from Florence:

"Again, the bronze horse may be taken in hand, which will be an immortal glory and eternal honor to the memory of the prince your father and the illustrious house of Sforza."

Leonardo reread his lengthy and carefully composed letter. The duke has told me himself, he agonized, that the equestrian statue cannot be considered in these uncertain times. Then how shall I earn my keep in Milan? Must I return to Florence to be the laughingstock of my old companions in Verrocchio's workshop? How often some of them envied my commissions for the pictures—which I never finished. I have always held my head high among my mates. They shall never see me again unless I return to Florence crowned with success.

He bit his lip; frowning, he penned his conclusion to his plea for patronage:

"And if any of the above-named things seem to anyone to be impossible or not feasible, I am most ready to make the experiment in your park, or in whatever place may please your Excellency—to whom I commend myself with the utmost humility."

Chapter 8

$\mathcal{P}$ERHAPS Duke Ludovico actually took the time necessary to study Leonardo's plans for a successful war. But as no hostilities developed the busy ruler showed no immediate interest in armored cars or portable bridges. He really desired to erect the equestrian memorial which his dead brother had planned over a decade ago and which would now add greatly to his own glory. But Il Moro was a man of many moods and desires.

Milan by the year 1483 had grown into one of the largest and wealthiest cities in all Europe. Surrounded by the richly productive farmlands of Lombardy, it had added to its vast revenues by planting groves of mulberry trees. The raising of silkworms, which fed on these trees, and the weaving of costly fabrics meant employment for thousands of workers. Another source for Milan's wealth was the manufacture of armor for both man and steed, as well as every known type of hand weapon.

Duke Ludovico should have had little difficulty in securing the necessary appropriations for the great bronze statue of his father. But at the time of Leonardo's arrival in Milan he seems to have been occupied in collecting his yearly revenue of six hundred thousand ducats for "personal expenses." At least half of this sum was spent on the servants and hangers-on of his sumptuous court and on his travels. For the duke liked to make his many journeys at the head of a veritable army of guards and secretaries, musicians, falconers, and grooms.

From the time he was sixteen Leonardo had wonderingly observed the luxurious living of the Medici and their circle. But never in Florence had he seen the lush extravagance which both astonished and repelled him in Milan. The duke and his favorites wore clothing of almost legendary magnificence and sparkled with priceless jewels. The exotic foods served at their feasts appeared in such superabundance that rarity became grossness. Every detail of the dinnerware was perfect: bowls of Murano glass; goblets of silver gilt, fashioned in quaint designs; serving platters and plates decorated with dolphins and mermaids and stories of the Grecian gods.

The total effect was overwhelming. Leonardo at the first of Il Moro's frequent feasts grew bedazzled with the lights from numerous candelabra and latticed Arabian lanterns. The odors from his neighbors' gold and enamel pomade balls sickened his stomach. He could not eat; he could not even enjoy the delicate music of the court musicians. Under eyelids heavy with fatigue, he watched the servants who passed from guest to guest with food and wine or bowls of sweet-scented water and embroidered napkins for their cleansing between the many courses.

A majority of the servitors were Italians, slender, deft of hand and light of foot. But here and there a slave, Moorish or Nubian, with his strange native garb and dark face, caught the diner's eye. The latter especially, or so it seemed to Leonardo, might have been chosen that their sooty complexions would by contrast enhance the whiteness of the court ladies' bosoms and shoulders. It hurt Leonardo to see these splendidly built men of Africa, shorn of their strength, bending with servility to pour the wine for a languid Milanese idler. Slaves! Leonardo had always detested the very thought of slavery. Now he sighed, for it was not so easy to free men as to open a cage of helpless birds bought in the market place.

Even more pitiful in their degradation, decided Leonardo, was the group of dwarfs Duke Ludovico had bidden to amuse the company. Some were merely men in miniature, insultingly like the courtiers to whom they sang their bawdy songs. But others were hardly more human in their pathetic ugliness than the apes and monkeys in Il Moro's zoo behind the castle. Now the smallest and most misshapen of all the unhappy monsters climbed with difficulty upon the high banquet table to perform a grotesque dance.

Leonardo shivered with disgust. The dwarf's frail body seemed wracked by his exertions; his eyes were bright with pain, perhaps disease. If, instead of exposing his deformity, he might only be sent into a decent obscurity to wait for the release death brings even to the lowest of animals caught in a trap! God help me, thought Leonardo suddenly, why do I pity him? For what am I but another servant of the court, ready to grimace and sing and dance when I catch my master's nod!

The artist forgot his rage and disgust as he wandered through Milan. He delighted in much that he saw, although it was easy to visualize how he might beautify the city once he had gained the duke's confidence. Leonardo admired the unfinished cathedral. But why should Italy call in German architects, he fumed. Ah, if I might be commissioned to draw plans for its completion . . . ! The *castello,* where the young duke and putative ruler of Lombardy lived in royal loneliness with no friends but his horses and his hunting hounds, was, like the city, excellently fortified. Leonardo longed to lighten its gloom with the beauty of a Florentine villa. Passing before the pink houses with their red roofs and Gothic windows, he dreamed of himself as the court architect who might transform all Milan.

But such preferment lay in the future. For the first few years after his arrival in Milan Leonardo suffered the galling uncertainty of a hanger-on at Duke Ludovico's court. He soon gave up all hope of serving Il Moro as military engineer. When that post became vacant it was given to another. Perhaps the duke had not enough imagination to be intrigued by the plans for more efficient warfare which Leonardo had spread before him. It might have been different had he been sorely pressed by Milan's enemies. But the tyrant of Milan, like the tyrant of Florence, decided to depend upon the wiles of diplomacy rather than on improved cannon and scaling ladders.

Leonardo had slightly stressed his abilities as an artist, compared to his gifts as a military expert. Il Moro seemed to consider him primarily as a musician and a painter. There were no wartime occupations for Leonardo. Milan, at peace with its neighbors, offered a cold welcome to Florentine craftsmen.

The savings Leonardo da Vinci had brought from Florence were so sadly diminished that he could no longer keep even a humble roof over his head. Fortunately he gained the friendship of the Milanese artist, Ambrogio de Predis. Ambrogio, in his late twenties, had become court painter to the ducal family.

Before long the two received a commission for an altarpiece. Leonardo was instructed to paint the Virgin and Child in the center panel; Ambrogio, four angels on the altar wings.

For the first time Leonardo felt happy in Milan. In the spring of 1483 he feasted his eyes and restored his soul on the beauties of the countryside around the city. He spent hours studying and drawing flowers before he was ready to paint them beneath the feet of his "Virgin of the Rocks." The grotto, which formed the Madonna's background, was dark and mysterious, for Leonardo never forgot the awesome cave he had discovered during his boyhood days at Vinci.

The "Virgin of the Rocks" was not finished on the agreed date! The members of the brotherhood who had ordered the altarpiece felt justifiably aggrieved at the delay, especially as Leonardo had managed to forget a number of their suggestions. They withheld payment. Fortunately the Florentine had by this time found other means of supporting himself.

The princes and wealthy gentlemen of Milan were far less generous than the aristocracy of Florence in commissioning statues and paintings for the beautification of their city. But many of them were as eager to have portraits painted of themselves or of members of their household as Leonardo's neighbors had been in Vinci. Duke Ludovico was no exception; Ambrogio de Predis had already painted the likeness of one of the court musicians as well as a certain high-spirited Sforza princess. Now, occupied with another aristocratic model, he suggested to Ludovico that Leonardo be commissioned to paint Cecilia Gallerani.

Cecilia had won Ludovico's love in her early youth and beauty; now she still triumphed over her rivals for the duke's fickle favor. The duke, although coarse in his tastes and irresponsible in character, had scholarly tastes. Even more than Cecilia's rare beauty he valued her fine mind and real accomplishments, for she spoke Latin fluently, sang, was a gifted musician, and wrote poetry.

Leonardo had already imprisoned on canvas the mystery of the young girl's large eyes, the half-mockery of her smile. For surely the angel kneeling in proud indifference before the "Virgin of the Rocks" was the duke's cherished mistress. Her provocative smile was intensified in the portrait of the most beautiful woman he was destined ever to paint, the "Lady with the Weasel."

Many of the courtiers who first looked admiringly on the portrait believed it was an ermine Cecilia held in her arms. For, strangely enough, the little creature, fabled to suffer death rather than stain its innocent whiteness, was Ludovico's favorite symbol.

Then Leonardo da Vinci found an occupation even more agreeable than painting lovely ladies or altarpieces. He was given the title of General Artificier and Architect for the Court of Milan, and Il Moro made sure that Leonardo earned his salary—which was often in arrears.

Since the Florentine could easily qualify as an engineering expert, he was frequently sent on journeys to inspect the canals and waterways of Lombardy. Some of the canals he built for Duke Ludovico's country estates were instrumental in drying up the swampy ground and made cultivation possible; he also devised a practical scheme of transforming the turbulent Adige River into a navigable waterway terminating in Lake Como.

As architect Leonardo was ordered to draw plans for the dome of the still unfinished cathedral of Milan; later he was sent as one of the consultants who were to design the cathedral at Pavia. Here, he added much to his knowledge by hours of reading in the spacious, quiet library of Duke Gian's castle.

Again he grew restless; again, as in Florence, a heavy calamity seemed at first to offer him opportunities for his varied talents. For several years a plague had raged in Italy; it now struck Milan with peculiar virulence. Usually Duke Ludovico trusted his court astrologers implicitly, but now he ignored their conclusions that this terrible sickness was caused by the evil influence of certain stars and could not be subdued. The duke ordered that the stricken should be isolated; he donated thirty thousand ducats for a huge hospital where they might be quarantined. When such measures failed to arrest the plague, Il Moro left Milan and the pestilence behind him.

He sought refuge on one of his country estates. No one from the plague-infested area was allowed to approach him. Even after they had been well-aired and perfumed, he trembled with fear when he felt obliged to read important state papers which were sent to him from Milan.

Meanwhile Leonardo neither ate nor slept. The plague had planted an amazing idea in his fertile brain and he was like a man possessed until he had sketched or written out his ideas for combating this recurrent evil. The duke might save himself and his court favorites by retiring to a safe distance; but what about the commoners "packed together like goats," jostling each other in the refuse-littered streets?

Employing that charm which had won him many a favor in the past, Leonardo persuaded a high court official to allow him to accompany the messenger who kept the duke in touch with affairs in Milan. When they arrived at the country estate it was a simple matter to induce Mona Cecilia to smuggle Leonardo and the latest of his notebooks into Ludovico's presence.

The duke was friendly but not overly cordial. He did not allow Leonardo to approach close enough to kiss his hand; as they talked the hypochondriac sniffed again and again at his scent ball, gold, set with rubies and pearls. The perfume, although probably not potent enough to kill any infection Leonardo might have carried with him, was still sufficiently strong to make the artist, who hated heavy scents, rather ill.

"It was good of you to come to cheer me in my loneliness," lied the royal exile. "Did you bring your lute? No? Then, alas, you cannot join us in a little concert we planned for this evening."

"But I have brought your grace these notes and drawings," answered Leonardo da Vinci. He handed the book to a waiting page, gorgeous in red and gold; the youth knew better than to hand it to his master.

"Ah, yes. A new project you could not bear to wait to discuss until I return to Milan?" The duke's voice had grown a little sharp. "I shall look it over when the pages are properly aired and treated. I must be doubly careful of my health since Venus is now in the ascent," he confided.

Leonardo, who hated astrologers and their quackery with all his heart, restrained a sarcastic smile.

"I wonder whether my lord would care to rival Boccaccio in his fame?" he asked smoothly.

The duke stared at him uneasily. What had the great Florentine storyteller to do with Leonardo's unauthorized visit?

"If I win any laurels it will not be as a writer but as the father of my people," he answered modestly.

"I need not remind you that the Black Death of a hundred years ago brought together certain ladies and gentlemen seeking to escape from the plague. And the tales they told to relieve their boredom now delight us as the *Decameron*."

"Still, I do not see . . ."

"If your grace, after a study of my plans, will act to avert another plague from Milan," explained Leonardo, "your name will also be coupled with this devastating sickness, even as men remember Boccaccio and the Black Death."

After what he considered a safe interval Duke Ludovico carefully studied the notebook Leonardo had brought him from Milan. In words and line drawings Leonardo had described the model cities he urged the Milanese ruler to build. These ten cities, he suggested, would have a limited population of thirty thousand inhabitants, each with five thousand houses to accommodate them. These towns would be erected along the banks of a river or on the seashore. For, by the ingenious construction of sewers, garbage flung into the streets and the filth from stables and privies could be washed away into the river or the sea.

He explained the method by which these cities would be free of smoke, how the width of the streets would be proportioned to the height of the houses. Every room in these comfortable dwellings would be filled with light and fresh air that flowed through the round bay windows. The architect even included such details as plans for a comfortable living room and suggestions on how to deliver wood and food supplies without disturbing the houseowner.

Of course, these houses were intended only for the rich! The poor were to be kept in their proper place, literally a lower stratum of the city's structure. For them Leonardo planned a second city beneath the first. No noisy porters, no creaking carts would be allowed to disturb the aristocrats above; below, the workers could trade and toil and sweat that their masters might remain comfortable and well-fed. If the populace benefited from the sanitary measures installed for their masters, so much the better.

Ludovico had lacked the imagination to see the value of Leonardo da Vinci's suggestions for a more ruthlessly efficient method of war. Now he made no attempt to visualize the dream cities sketched in the Florentine's notebooks. It would take a dozen fortunes, he told his Cecilia, yawning over the last of the drawings, and to what end? Could you expect a servant to refrain from sweeping into the street the bones left from yesterday's supper? Or a gentleman from spitting whenever he felt a tickling in the throat? Then why this bother of washed streets and a system of locks that the river might take care of the polluted water?

And so the ten model cities, like so many of Leonardo's dreams, remained hidden in his notebooks until the dawning of a brighter day. He was not too disappointed; for after the first frenzy of setting down his plans, he realized that it was not likely his patron would welcome such radical ideas. At least, he decided, I can do a little to decrease the smell of filth about Milan!

By the time all danger of the plague was over and Duke Ludovico was again installed in his palace, Leonardo was ready to show him more plans for the sanitation of his city. One of these was an improved toilet seat, guaranteed by the inventor to close tightly. Other improvements concerned the ducal stables, which, Leonardo daringly asserted, could be kept sweet-smelling and clean.

"Let the stable be divided into three arched compartments," he explained. "The middle one will house the groom, who must always guard your valuable steeds; the ones on either side will be for the horses. Beneath the floor of the middle room will run two channels into which all the refuse from the floors may pass."

At last Il Moro became really interested. He considered himself a modern man who welcomed modern ideas. Also, he was very fond of his horses.

Chapter 9

LIKE the duke, his master, Leonardo loved horses. Some of his happiest hours in Milan were spent in the regal stables Ludovico had established for his favorites: Arabians, with delicate ankles, as nervous as a witch on a broomstick, yet obedient to the slightest touch, and therefore much esteemed for hunting; war horses from Barbary, strong enough to bear not only their own protective armor but a mail-clad rider; beauties bred in Sicily and Thrace for the duke's pleasure.

Leonardo made sketch after sketch of the proud and lovely creatures. When one died the artist pretended to perform an autopsy to prove that the beast had not been poisoned by a revengeful groom. But Leonardo, although well-pleased to have saved the suspected varlet from the hangman, was really interested in dissecting the animal. The dissections he had performed on animals and even on human cadavers in the hospital at Florence had verified for him Verrocchio's belief that the painter and the sculptor must study anatomy. He felt he must know every muscle, every sinew of the stallion he still hoped to cast in bronze as a memorial to Francesco Sforza.

Duke Ludovico had a brain which fluttered from project to project as lightly as a humming bird from red to white rosebush in the *castello* gardens. But, somehow, if an idea once lodged in his mind, he never entirely forgot it. Leonardo on coming to Milan had in the ardor of his own enthusiasm, caused Ludovico to lose interest in the colossal horse and rider. The duke, puzzled by the Florentine's babble of the hundred thousand pounds of bronze required, of five huge furnaces for casting, had decided that the memorial might be deferred for a few years.

But in 1489 the duke decided to take up the matter again. He forgot that he had ever discussed the proposed equestrian statue with Leonardo da Vinci! Completely ignoring Leonardo, he sent a request to Lorenzo de' Medici for sculptors who might be commissioned to begin the work. The duke believed he had detected the flaw in Leonardo's character. Something of a genius, perhaps, he decided, but a man whose ideas ranged from improved scaling ladders to stable drains was too impractical to be entrusted with an important commission.

Fortunately for Leonardo his rivals from Florence also failed to gain Il Moro's contract for the memorial statue.

Meanwhile Leonardo da Vinci enjoyed the duke's half-hearted support for his lute-playing and occasional pictures. His "Lady with the Weasel" brought him better fortune than the contemporary "Virgin of the Rocks," although the latter really influenced a new school of painters in Milan. For during her sittings for Leonardo, Mona Cecilia had learned to appreciate the painter's keen wit and unique philosophy. She invited Leonardo to attend the group of scholars and culture-loving courtiers over which she presided. The lady's patronage and her influence over Ludovico made it possible for Leonardo to improve his position in court circles.

Leonardo had done much to make up for his early neglect of his studies in Vinci. His reading was wide and what he read he digested and always remembered. Now in spite of his defective education he was able to gain the respect of the learned men of Milan. And how the ladies admired him! In a moment he could sketch the sweetest pattern of flowers or birds on a fair one's scent box; or illustrate with fantastic creatures described in the Bestiary a damsel's favorite fable; or design for the duke's latest fete a dress so strangely beautiful that every one of the wearer's friends was ready to swoon with envy.

One of Leonardo's greatest triumphs was a cloak which made Mona Cecilia even more beautiful to the duke's admiring eyes. The snowy feathers which floated gracefully at Cecilia's slightest movement made her resemble the proud swans which swam in the *castello's* moat; like the pampered birds, the lady wore about her long, white neck a collar decorated with pearls. Il Moro, a poet as well as a shrewd observer of feminine finery, was charmed. He agreed with Cecilia that Leonardo should be put in charge of the pageantry to honor the marriage of Duke Gian Galeazzo.

Although Ludovico had usurped the young ruler's prerogatives one after the other, he still hesitated to proclaim himself ruler over Milan. His nephew was weak and sickly; if he died without an heir, Uncle Ludovico, his hands still clean, would step into his place. But Gian, although he passed from puny youth into puny manhood, refused to die. Now, in 1490, Ludovico called Leonardo da Vinci before him to plan the marriage ceremonials of Duke Gian Galeazzo to Isabella, princess of Aragona.

This granddaughter of the king of Naples was as tall and proud and stately as the beautiful princess in a fairy tale; her bridegroom was thin and pale and bore himself more like a frightened commoner than a youth of noble birth. They had not sought one another in love as lesser folk may do; they had been betrothed when children, for their marriage was an affair of state, which, it was hoped, would strengthen the friendship between Naples and Milan.

So on this day of pomp and pride, Isabella stood in her stiffly flaring brocaded robes as cold and lifeless as the doll-like madonna which is carried at the head of the procession when the church calendar records a feast; while Gian, his hand limp between her jeweled fingers, wished he were safe in his own quiet chamber with only his hunting hounds to keep him company.

The holiday crowds cheered the bridal pair, and, loud with wine, called the heavens to witness the beauty of the bride and the gallantry of her husband. But Leonardo, the last preparations for the evening's festivities completed, looked on the pair with pity for their youth and helplessness.

In the court ball that evening Isabella seemed to forget her royal dignity. Her skirts of gold brocade whirled about her as she performed a Neapolitan dance. She was followed by maskers in appropriate costumes who presented the dances of their native countries: Spain, Poland, Hungary, Germany and France. There were even Turks who dashed into the hall on horseback with a great clattering of hoofs.

Now, Isabella of Aragona, no longer a royal bride but a happy child, clapped her hands with delight; she laughed shrilly at the antics of the court jester, who mocked the dancers as he pranced between them. Yet Gian never smiled but stared morosely at the heavy curtain of glowing satin which hung at one end of the vast hall.

It was almost midnight before this curtain rose on the masque Leonardo da Vinci had devised as an ending for the wedding festivities.

"The masque is called 'Paradiso,' " Duke Ludovico whispered to Isabella.

"It is so beautiful," she murmured, her eyes brimming with sudden tears. "If heaven is so fair, and I am worthy, I wish I might die this very night and enter its gates." She spoke extravagantly; but in the tragic years that stretched before her the princess often remembered and wished, indeed, that she might have died that night.

Only a genius who combined within himself the imagination of an artist and the ingenuity of a mechanic could have devised such a setting. High above the stage a gilded heaven twinkling with stars seemed to stretch into infinity. Behind panes of glass appeared the signs of the zodiac etched in flickering lights. Below loomed gigantic statues to which the actors concealed within gave the semblance of motion; these seven heroic figures represented the seven known planets, each moving in its own orbit.

So much for the beauties of Paradiso! On either side, at a lower level, artificial fires and terror-inspiring monsters suggested the depths of hell. The spectacle reminded the awed audience of the murals they had so often seen in church, portraying the eternal abodes of the blessed and the damned. But this seemed so frightfully real!

As though to calm the more timorous, there came the sound of music sweetly played in the distance. Leonardo had devised an artificial stream of water which flowed around the base of the stage. Now there appeared upon the river's surface little boats, decorated with flowers and filled with singers and lute-players. Many wondered that they heard so clearly the music and the speech of the actors upon the stage. Leonardo, who had studied the acoustic value of water, might have told them that his "river," as well as the artfully planned dome above it, magnified and clarified the mingled sounds.

Bellincioni, a Florentine poet, had written the masque in which Apollo and Jupiter and the seven Christian Virtues joined to pay due honor to the young duke's bride. As Il Moro had furnished the writer with most of the very conventional plot, he considered himself a co-author and the masque a miracle of beauty and good taste. He was so pleased at the praises heaped upon him after the performance that he was actually willing to share his honors with Leonardo da Vinci.

"I could not believe my own eyes when I saw those stars fading and the nymphs floating through the air," the duke complimented Leonardo. "Is it a secret of your craft, or may you tell me what miracle you employed?"

Leonardo bowed. "Pulleys," he answered briefly before he turned away to direct the workmen as they prepared to demolish his handiwork. For Duke Ludovico feared that some lesser mortal than Milan's ruler might try to reproduce his precious masque; even during the performance he had decided that the costly scenery and the ingenious devices which were Leonardo's secret must be destroyed together.

Fortunately for Leonardo da Vinci the respect and admiration he had won from his patron with his presentation of "Paradiso" did not disappear with the destruction of the gilded dome and the heroic figures that represented the planets. Ludovico continued to sing the Florentine's praises.

Then, on a certain spring day, three months after the young duke's marriage, Leonardo completed one of his notebooks and began another. His first entry ran: "On the twenty-third day of April 1490 I commenced this book and commenced the horse."

Chapter 10

$\mathcal{A}$LL his life it was Leonardo's misfortune never to be allowed to concentrate on a single piece of work. Hardly had he completed his final designs for the colossal horse when he was obliged to design decorations for the streets of Milan and masquerade costumes for the festivities in honor of Ludovico's own marriage.

For Il Moro, after a long and merry bachelorhood, had ended the tiresome diplomatic negotiations that had blocked his marriage to Beatrice d'Este. Less than a year after the nuptial ceremonies of young Duke Gian and the granddaughter of the king of Naples, visitors of high degree began to crowd into Milan to celebrate an even gaudier bridal. Some of the noble guests, including Beatrice's clever, domineering sister, Isabella of Mantua, complained of the overcrowding. Ludovico was apologetic. Some of the envoys even, he explained, had to be accommodated in humble inns. But in spite of the midwinter cold no one would suffer, for the peasants had brought into Milan plenty of firewood; as for food—why, even now the oxen stumbled along the roads, slippery with ice, to bring the choicest of meats and fowls and game for Milan's distinguished guests.

Leonardo da Vinci had completed the last of the fantastic costumes for the three-day tourney which had been planned in the bride's honor. Now he was privileged to meet Beatrice d'Este, a girl of fifteen, who gave him a pudgy hand to kiss and listened with a sulky smile to his courtly phrases. Weary from her journey, bewildered by the tumult that had brought into Milan the unseemly confusion of a carnival, the bride cloaked her doubts and fears with a haughty hostility. Leonardo feared that she would never be happy in Milan. He shrugged his shoulders; the marital woes which seemed to loom ahead for Il Moro were no concern of the court artificer. He hurried back to his workshop, for he remembered that a helmet, designed for one of the knights in the tourney, was missing. And he himself must see that the triumphal arch he had designed for the vast ballroom was well-braced. It was decorated with a portrait of the bridegroom's warrior father, Francesco Sforza, seated upon a prancing steed—one of the preliminary studies Leonardo had made for the bronze statue.

The Florentine's studio and workshop now occupied a modest corner of Ludovico's palace. Leonardo da Vinci's students and apprentices were promising young artists who revered their brilliant master and were proud to be known as members of his *bottega*. To these youths Leonardo tried to give the inspired tutelage he had known in the days of his own apprenticeship to Verrocchio. Only lately news had come to him of his teacher's death. He was the only real father I ever knew, Leonardo thought in his first grief. He always had such high hopes for my future. But what have I accomplished? What have I done with my life?

As soon as Leonardo crossed the threshold of his studio an apprentice rushed to him with a story of the latest misdeeds of the imp Giacomo. If Leonardo had shared the superstition of his contemporaries, even the most learned, he would have agreed that the ten-year-old boy was in truth the offspring of a witch and her demon lover.

Less than a year before, Leonardo, usually so cold in his personal relationships, had taken the child not only into his workshop but into his heart. Giacomo's father was too poor to pay the fee usually required at the beginning of a youth's apprenticeship. In fact, the family were in such desperate circumstances that Leonardo, quite spoiled by luxurious living, shuddered when he remembered the meal he had been forced to share under their wretched roof. There were maggots in the cheese; the oil which dressed the salad was rancid. No wonder that little Giacomo, when permitted to eat at Leonardo's table, not only gobbled up three times his share, but later outraged the cook by stealing dainties from her cupboard.

He had come to Leonardo's household wearing ragged trousers, a filthy shirt, and torn shoes. Leonardo had supplied him immediately with a complete and tasteful outfit; he warned Giacomo, as he strutted about in his new finery, that these were not castoffs purchased from a huckster of secondhand garments, and must be cared for tenderly. Giacomo smiled and promised to keep the handsome suit and the hat with its jaunty feathers as clean and whole as though they were a saint's mantle, only brought from its wrappings on a feast day. Before the end of the week he had torn his embroidered jacket, hopelessly stained his linen shirt, and lost one of his shoes. At the end of the year Leonardo, who for all his recklessness in money matters, kept his accounts as carefully as his father, the notary, had set down in black and white that he had purchased twenty-four pairs of shoes for his young protégé.

On one of the occasions when Leonardo recorded in his notebooks the personal trivia of his everyday life, he described the boy as "thievish, lying, obstinate, greedy . . . he stole money from the wallet, and it was never possible to make him confess, although I was absolutely convinced. . . . Giacomo had supper for two and did mischief for four, for he broke three flagons, spilt the wine. . . . He stole a pencil worth twenty-two *soldi* from Mardo who was with me. It was of silver."

Leonardo seemed to have borne the rascal's pranks with the love and patience of a too-indulgent father. Although Giacomo showed little talent and soon took his place in the studio as the master's personal attendant rather than artist-apprentice, Leonardo continually pampered him and dressed him like a young prince. Giacomo, irresponsible, lazy, and often insolent, showed no gratitude nor did Leonardo da Vinci look to him for either obedience or affection. Leonardo loved beauty in flower and cloud and maid and youth; it was enough for him that Giacomo was very beautiful.

Today the master listened patiently as the apprentice told his sorry tale.

"The costumes you designed for the 'wild men' in tonight's festival! Some of the gentlemen came to try them on and one of them left his purse with his own garments upon a couch. No one saw Giacomo take it. . . ."

"Of course not," Leonardo agreed with a weary sigh. "The lad is not only as mischievous but as quick as Il Moro's pet monkey."

"We found the purse hidden under the little rascal's shirt. Empty! He must have spent all the money for sweetmeats or cakes, for during the past hour he has twice been sick. Now, what shall be done with Giacomo?" he ended breathlessly.

"Put him to bed and see that he does not overload his stomach at supper," advised Leonardo.

"But first, he should be well-beaten, and if the master will permit me. . . . "

"The master suggests that you should recite the rosary of your own sins before you sit in judgment on Giacomo," said Leonardo so sternly that the apprentice shivered and wondered how the master, seemingly blind, had discovered. . . . "I think the boy is punished enough if he is still too sick to enjoy Il Moro's celebration tomorrow."

But Giacomo, whose stomach, like his conscience, never bothered him with more than a temporary indisposition, made such a rapid recovery that the next morning he was ready to bathe and dress and attend the glittering festival. Clinging to his master's hand, the boy stamped his feet, clapped his hands, and shouted so loudly in his excitement that many spectators turned to look at him. He was well worth their scrutiny with his gently curved, graceful body, his large, soft eyes, and abundant curls. No wonder that Leonardo, who had painted him again and again, looked down on the child so proudly and tried to forget his misdemeanors.

The "wild men," whose sensational but hardly authentic costumes Leonardo had devised, dashed past on their plunging horses. The saddlecloth of the leader's steed was woven of gold thread and embroidered with a design of peacock's eyes. On his intricately fashioned helmet Leonardo had placed a peacock mounted on a golden ball. The artificer took the trouble to record in his notebook of this period that the golden sphere represented the earth, the eyes of the proud peacock the beauty of those who are loyal servants of their liege lord. The mirror he had inserted in the knight's shield, added Leonardo, taught that the man who desired recognition must be mirrored in his own virtues.

Thus he tried to dignify his ephemeral productions by adorning his efforts with the pretty and playful allegories of his day. But he sometimes wondered with sudden savagery why he should spend hours on a foolish helmet, perhaps to be worn once before it was cast aside. His fingers itched to work on the bronze horse; or his brain to devise still another improvement in the great wings which lay hidden in a corner of his workshop.

Many helmets were decorated with the head of a savage Moor in compliment to the bridegroom's nickname; some of the knights carried the allusion further and daubed their faces with brown paint. The mantles of the knights challenged in their warm colors the flashing brocades of the rival duchesses, Isabella of Aragona and Beatrice d'Este and the ladies who surrounded them, flaunting their loveliness like a rose garden in spring.

But roses for all their beauty, once they have reached their bloom, droop and scatter their fragrant petals to the wind. When the three-day tourney ended, the knights put aside their armor and fantastic helmets and shields; the ladies, surfeited with sweetmeats and excitement, languidly drew their traveling cloaks about them and settled themselves in their coaches for their homeward journey. Isabella of Aragona who had wearied the wedding guests with tales of the beauty and intelligence of her very young son, Francesco, hurried home to gloat over the gilded cradle in the ducal palace at Pavia; her husband, young Duke Gian, even paler and thinner of late, rejoiced in his reunion with his hounds and horses.

Duke Ludovico, a little jaded from too heavy and too frequent feasting, asked his royal artificer, Leonardo da Vinci, whether he had started work on a long-delayed project, a painting of "The Last Supper." But first, he suggested, would Leonardo confer with Duchess Beatrice? Mona Cecilia, said the duke, sighing over the unreasonableness of women, had flaunted at the wedding feast the "swan cloak" Leonardo had designed, and now the duchess insisted . . .

"She will not be satisfied with a mere duplicate," explained Duke Ludovico. "But if you improve upon the original, how will we be able to appease Mona Cecilia?" The duke raised his weary eyes as though appealing to the heavens to answer him in his perplexity. "How can one ever satisfy a woman?" asked Ludovico.

Chapter 11

$\mathcal{B}$EATRICE D'ESTE, as Leonardo learned during their first conference on cloaks, was not easily satisfied. Scarcely suggesting womanhood in face and body, the chubby little duchess had the character of a spoiled child. Although not as clever and well-read as her sister Isabella of Mantua, Beatrice had benefited from a classical education. She knew something of the Latin poets and even had a smattering of philosophy. But of what use was philosophy when she felt homesick and alien in Milan and was convinced that the entire world had turned against her?

She hated Isabella of Aragona whose child, if he lived to maturity, would surely be duke of Milan. Duchess Isabella was not a lady to show any consideration for a rival; whenever the two met, not only the sensitive Gian but his thick-skinned uncle feared their wives might actually come to blows. Beatrice hated her second rival almost as sorely. Ludovico insisted on Cecilia Gallerani maintaining her former apartments in the *castello*. He saw no reason, he said, why the two could not become friends. Cecilia tried to play a conciliatory part but Beatrice grew more and more spiteful. When she learned that Leonardo had painted her beautiful rival she considered that a sufficient reason for hating the artist, too.

Beatrice loved hunting passionately but even more she loved dancing and masques. To her the greatest genius of his day was nothing more than a court servant to design carnival costumes or to plan and construct the setting of a masque Bellincioni had just written for her amusement. She rewarded the artist with careless praise although the court went into raptures over his device of mechanical birds which appeared to fly above the stage. Beatrice in her feline cruelty seemed to know that while Leonardo's hands constructed these toys to be broken and cast aside after an evening's pleasure, his spirit roamed in a world she might never enter. Although she had heard only rumors of a strange machine "with wings," she knew from her husband's jeering that the Florentine longed to be free to carry out his many daring plans. She sensed Leonardo's cold contempt for the fripperies he manufactured at her bidding and hated him the more.

Now not only the trivial tasks Leonardo despised but serious obligations crowded his waking hours and caused him to toss wakefully in his troubled bed. At last the duke seemed really impatient to see the model for the equestrian statue completed. Il Moro also agreed with the prior of Santa Maria della Grazie that the artist should be ready to show more than preliminary sketches for "The Last Supper" which had long been promised for the convent's refectory wall.

Duke Ludovico had seen and admired the lamp Leonardo had sketched for him with a globe of water about its base to magnify the rays. He had glanced over other sketches which had intrigued him greatly, such as plans for improved irrigation for the farmlands beyond Milan. Surely, thought Ludovico, such a versatile workman must be allowed to plan and ponder and tinker in peace.

But the next day Beatrice would persuade her husband that no one but Leonardo could please her with a new curtain for her next spectacle. Or she might report to the duke with a childish pout: "Your pet, Leonardo, has just installed pipes in Isabella's bathroom at Pavia. Cold *and* hot water! While I, your wife, must sit in my tub and be frozen or scalded while my stupid maids empty their pitchers over me. When will Leonardo find time to pipe heated water for my comfort?"

"But, my darling," pleaded Ludovico, "if you will only be patient and permit . . ."

But patience had never been one of the little lady's virtues. The colossal statue and "The Last Supper" mural were postponed while Leonardo fitted pipes for Beatrice's bathroom.

Even when Beatrice was too engrossed with hunting or refurbishing her fabulous wardrobe to make demands upon him, Leonardo neglected his commissions. He spent hours studying the plants he brought home from his lonely excursions; or sitting with his pupils, he discussed philosophy or told stories; or added new memoranda to his bulging notebooks. For days he sought escape in the pleasant world of mechanics and mathematics. One who knew him well in Milan wrote to a friend: "He is entirely wrapped up in geometry and has no patience for painting." While another contemporary commented: "His mechanical experiments have made painting so distasteful to him that he cannot even bear to take up a brush."

The writers exaggerated. Like so many mere spectators they could not share the artist's "impatience," not with his art but with himself for his failure to produce. Leonardo might allow weeks to pass without mounting the scaffold hung at one end of the refectory of Santa Maria; but in his notebooks on the very pages covered with mechanical designs and mathematical formula he sketched now the head of a young apostle or the haunted face of Judas.

In selecting "The Last Supper" as the subject for the mural Leonardo was commissioned to paint for the convent, Duke Ludovico had chosen one of the favorite subjects of the Renaissance painters. Before Leonardo they had all been content to follow a conventional pattern; on one side of the table they portrayed Jesus with his eleven devoted disciples grouped about him. Set apart by his wickedness, Judas crouched in lonely ignominy.

Years before in Florence the youthful Leonardo da Vinci had made preliminary sketches of the subject. One study closely followed the familiar pattern, for Judas sat alone on the nearer side of the table. But now a daring thought seized the artist: what a triumph it would be to place the arch-traitor with the faithful disciples; to show by their withdrawal that they already guessed who was the accursed one among them!

Leonardo began to search for models for the trusted disciples, Judas and Jesus. Sometimes a face in the market place would attract the artist; he would study the stranger's features until he had memorized them; transfer the remembered countenance on a sketching pad or notebook; study, revise—and usually reject. The study for the head of Judas, sketched in red chalk was done from a model with sharp, tense features and beardless; but in the finished masterpiece the dark menace of the face became intensified by a heavy beard.

Seated beside the loving and beloved disciple John, Leonardo's Judas seemed the embodiment of all evil. It was cruel of the painter to say, even in jest, when the prior of Santa Maria complained of his slowness in completing the picture, that if he could not find a suitable criminal in the slums of Milan for a model, he might be forced to ask the prior to sit for the portrait of Judas!

There were new difficulties when at last Leonardo felt ready to paint the central figure of his tragedy. He searched despairingly among the well-born youths of Milan; it never occurred to the son of a servant girl that the face of Jesus, himself a carpenter, might be suggested by some sturdy peasant or workman in the market place.

One evening Leonardo showed the sketches he had made of the two disciples, Philip and James the Elder, to a brother artist, Bernardino Zenale.

"I am satisfied with these; but where will I find my model for Jesus?" Leonardo asked his friend.

Bernardino Zenale looked long and admiringly upon the sketches before he answered. "You have made a grave mistake," he said at last. "The faces of these mortal men show such divine beauty, how can you ever hope to exceed them with a portrayal of the Son of God Himself?"

But Leonardo continued in his search. At first he found the model for Christ's hands. Later the artist jotted in the current notebook: "Christ, the young count—that of Cardinal del Mortaro." The young nobleman, shown in a preliminary sketch, was touchingly frail with drooping eyelids and a pensive mouth. There was something pitiful about the remoteness of this study, as though the model sensed he was, like so many youths of his day, doomed to premature illness and death. Or did he merely feel set apart and consecrated because Leonardo da Vinci had chosen him for this unique honor?

The majority of those who passed through the refectory of Santa Maria to see the long-awaited mural never dreamed of Leonardo's long search to achieve perfection in at least one of his works. How could they know of his search for models satisfactory even to his critical eye; of the hours he had spent mixing his paints that the colors might not suffer during the dampness and frost of a Milanese winter; of the heartbreaking difficulty of fitting thirteen figures into a convincing pattern behind a narrow table? Only a few artists knew and understood and marveled.

But Duke Ludovico swelled with pride as he viewed his munificent gift to his favorite church. He had not paid Leonardo his salary for some months but debts never troubled this generous patron of the arts. The prior tried to forget the unkind remark about himself attributed to the artist; he pointed out that even if Judas sat with the others, he looked so much the villain that he did not need to hold the moneybag which usually identified him. The monks beamed at the new glory that had come to their convent. The common folk nudged one another as they insisted they recognized several of the faces behind the long table.

"Eh, that one in the blue cloak, leaning over and pointing with his hands! I tell you he's the very image of Matthew, the tailor." "John? I ought to know him when his father's got a stall across from mine and I see him every market day!" Or a woman might cry out in deepest admiration: "Will you look at the tablecloth!

See, the fine blue borders. But some worthless man must have put it away in the linen chest after it was washed. No woman would ever have made those creases in the front."

Leonardo's pupils both admired and understood. He was a kind master but an indifferent teacher. He was kind, he was patient, but his visions blinded him to everything but his own work. Some of the youths who studied painting under Leonardo in Milan might have possessed the divine fire but it was quenched under the torrent of the master's genius. Not one of them ever became a true creator; they could only admire their friend and try to imitate his work.

With the exception of his pet and torment, Giacomo, and, later, the gently bred Francesco Melzi, he always remained coldly aloof from men and women alike. At times a veritable thinking-machine, Leonardo da Vinci had no need for love or companionship.

> If you are alone [he wrote], you belong only to yourself. If you are accompanied even by one companion you belong only half to yourself, or even less in proportion to the thoughtlessness of his conduct. If you must have companionship [he made the grudging concession], choose it from your studio; it may then help you to obtain the advantages which result from different methods of study.

In theory, however, Leonardo da Vinci had few superiors as an instructor. His conclusions on painting were at the same time brilliant and profound. He was eager to share these ideas with others and planned to collect everything he had written on the subject and to publish it, for the benefit of other artists, under the title, *Treatise on Painting*. He worked on the treatise for many years; but like so many of his pioneer ideas on anatomy and mechanics, his philosophy of art lay buried in the notebooks that were to be forgotten for centuries after his death.

But even though Leonardo's fellow-artists were not privileged to study his unpublished treatise, they learned many of his principles from his pictures. He was the first among painters to present the union he urged between art and science. They admired his realism, his truthful representation of the human body, of beast, of tree and flower. They marveled at his perfect draftsmanship, his superb treatment of light and shadow.

Some of these painters wondered why Leonardo's work, with all its faultless detail and painfully planned mathematical balance, did not become cold and mechanical. But even his harshest critics were forced to confess that the artist was never lost in the scientist.

They wondered also by what curious twist he often rendered the mystical realistic, the commonplace supernatural. For, sometimes, his madonnas and his angels seemed almost too sweetly human; yet the trees that waved in the background could have grown from no earthly soil. And was it an accident, others asked, that so many of the faces Leonardo drew should reflect his own half-gentle, half-teasing smile which set a riddle for the spectator but refused to answer it? No one could be certain; but all agreed that the art like the life of Leonardo da Vinci would always remain an enigma.

Chapter 12

ON A mild April evening in the year 1493 Duke Ludovico gathered about him a group of his friends, including the choicest scholars of Milan. His duchess was absent; she suffered, she informed her husband, from one of the devastating headaches which, since the birth of their son and heir, Maximiliano, frequently tortured her. The duke knew that Beatrice had spent the afternoon playing tennis; he knew also that she had already invited a few of her favorite ladies-in-waiting to join her in her apartments for a game of cards that evening. Beatrice had lost none of the intellectual interests of her girlhood. But although she yearned to hear the scholarly discussion the duke had planned, she stubbornly remained at her card table. For Beatrice was sure that Cecilia would grace the duke's learned gathering; the little duchess was in no mood to watch her husband's favorite display her wit and scholarship.

"And they call her 'the new Sappho' because of her learning," Beatrice snapped to her youngest and latest attendant, the beautiful Lucrezia. "I would call her rather . . ." and she uttered a name that caused Lucrezia, so lately come to court, to blush furiously and look down at her hands. Her eyes fell on the ruby ring Duke

Ludovico had just given her; he had already promised that his favorite painter, Leonardo, would soon do her portrait. Lucrezia wondered whether the Florentine would make her as overpoweringly lovely as he had Cecilia when she had posed for him with a weasel in her arms.

The night had grown chilly; Ludovico's privileged guests were grateful for the high-heaped logs in the great marble fireplace in the duke's own apartments. Leonardo leaned back in his great chair, gilded and rich with tapestry, and examined with his usual intentness the faces ringed about his host.

Duke Ludovico, his dark, complacent face suggesting at once the boldness of the lion and the cunning of the fox, lounged beside Mona Cecilia; Leonardo thought that her eyelids, modestly lowered as she listened to Il Moro's chatter, were more eloquent than any other woman's speech. Near by, nervously erect, sat young Duke Gian. The painter noticed with a feeling of impersonal pity that of late the youth had grown even more pale and emaciated. If he allowed himself to relax and folded his thin hands across his breast, considered Leonardo, he might easily serve as model for the effigy on his tomb. And, of course, the sculptor would be instructed to show a favorite little hunting hound curled at his feet.

But in contrast to her sickly husband, Duchess Isabella of Aragona looked dangerously alive. Her black eyes lighted now on the face of a fellow guest, now on the potted rose tree at her elbow. They flitted over a mural that depicted the love story of Dido and Aeneas, but so swiftly that Leonardo was willing to swear she could not, if questioned, describe a single figure. Her little hands, never at rest, tormented the red rose she had just torn from its stem. The birth of her son, Francesco, acknowledged heir to the dukedom of Milan and the rich farmlands of Lombardy, had failed to bring her comfort and assurance. The child was now sleeping behind the iron-barred windows of his bedchamber. He was guarded by the faithful peasant woman who had nursed his father before him. But the duchess knew how little the protection of a devoted servant would avail against the dagger of a hired assassin.

On this April evening Il Moro's brother-in-law, Cardinal Ip-

polito d'Este, stately in his scarlet robes, at once amused and
irritated Leonardo by his courteous manner to Ambrogio da Rosate.
Even a prince of the church, decided Leonardo, deemed it worth
his while to show politeness to a boastful charlatan like Ambrogio.
Not satisfied with his post as professor at the university of Pavia,
the ignoramus had wheedled the duke into appointing him court
astrologer as well as his personal physician.

Leonardo eagerly welcomed the tardy arrival of Fra Luca Pacioli,
the eminent mathematician who continued his studies while wearing the robes of the Franciscan order. To the painter he was both
friend and teacher. Leonardo, largely self-taught, was grateful for
further instruction; Pacioli was so struck by the combination of
scientist and artist that he suggested Leonardo should draw the
plates for his still uncompleted treatise on "proportion." It was the
happiest of collaborations. Later in the introduction to his book,
Pacioli called Leonardo "the most honorable of all painters, investigator of perspective, architect, and musician, a man furnished
with all the virtues."

A moment after the mathematician's arrival Bernardo Bellincioni, the pet poet of the court of Milan, drifted languidly across the
threshold, and the circle of guests, which included several famous
scholars and churchmen, was complete. Ludovico made an impatient gesture.

"Must we wait till dawn for a dawdling messenger?" he exclaimed. "Let us have music." He turned toward Leonardo: "Or
you, perhaps, will tell us one of your clever tales? No!" and always
childishly changeable in his desires, he nodded to his court poet:
"Recite for us again the charming verses you composed on the birth
of our first-born son."

The duke glanced maliciously at Isabella of Aragona who pretended to ignore the thrust. Everyone present knew how Ludovico's
dynastic hopes had risen with the birth of his child. True, the
rightful duke of Milan still lived, and he also had a son . . . but if
Ludovico grew too impatient . . . The air was heavy with hatred
and suspicion. The peace-loving cardinal sighed with relief as a
lackey ushered a man in dusty garments into the room.

"At last! the messenger of our envoy to Venice," murmured the cardinal, grateful for interruption.

The envoy's servant bowed low before the duke.

"You will forgive me," he began. "As I was already delayed on the road, I felt I must not pause even to repair my disordered dress before I delivered my master's message."

Even Il Moro, usually insensitive to another's needs, noticed that the speaker staggered from fatigue and that he spoke with difficulty like one suffering from thirst.

"My servants will bring you refreshments," he said graciously. "Then you must rest after your long ride. But first," and he held out his hand, "your master's message."

Several of the guests, knowing why they had been summoned, forgot court etiquette in their eagerness to look over Il Moro's shoulder at the parchment.

" 'Tis only a copy of the original letter," the duke told them rather patronizingly. "A letter, so our envoy to Venice wrote my secretary, written by Christopher Columbus himself in Barcelona, and later copied and sent to Rome and Florence. Now," he spread out the sheets before him and paused dramatically, enjoying the impatience which had grown up around him, "now, who will read the words which we are the first in Milan to enjoy?"

"Leonardo da Vinci is the best reader among us," suggested Fra Pacioli.

"Oh yes, by all means Leonardo must read us the message from India!" Bellincioni spoke quickly so that no one should suspect he was feeling a little hurt at not being chosen.

Leonardo looked inquiringly at the duke, who nodded and placed the closely written sheets in the artist's hand. Everyone, except Duke Gian, who had fallen into a doze, drew his chair closer to the reader in order to catch every word. The court attendants tiptoed as near as they dared.

In his charmingly modulated voice, the voice of a musician, Leonardo read the first account to reach Milan of that strange voyage across the Sea of Darkness.

Almost breathless with interest, cardinal and mathematician, duke and poet, followed the story as exciting and incredible as the wildest romance. Rivers with sands heavy with gold . . . spicery . . . naked savages. All this not part of a tale spun by an irresponsible traveler but a sober account prepared for their majesties of Spain by the godfearing explorer they had honored with the title of Admiral of the Ocean Sea!

When Leonardo ended his reading, Cecilia sighed regretfully. "It is all so wonderful," she said, "and in your reading the story became even more thrilling. Those handsome, copper-colored men of the forests . . ."

Cardinal Ippolito d'Este nodded complacently.

"It is good that Queen Isabella has seen her pious wish fulfilled and that the gospel has been brought to those who sat in darkness. Only recently I heard from the queen's own chaplain that six of these . . . what? . . . ah, yes, Indians! . . . brought back by the admiral were actually baptized in Barcelona. He informed me that the king and queen and the Infante Don Juan graciously consented to act as godparents."

He raised his delicately arched eyebrows inquiringly.

"Did you speak?" he asked with unfailing politeness as Leonardo seemed to relieve his feelings with a sceptical grunt. "Or perhaps you don't believe that their majesties of Spain graciously . . ."

"I must believe the report since it came from the court chaplain, and who am I to dispute the word of a holy man?" Leonardo answered with equal politeness. "Even without his testimony I would believe that a lady as intelligent as Queen Isabella might in her zeal for the church take part in such a doubtful ceremony."

The cardinal rose to his feet; he had grown pale with anger.

"You dare call the holy sacrament of baptism doubtful?" he thundered at Leonardo.

"How could a faithful son of the church be guilty of such sacrilege? I hope I may always rely on a powerful friend's protection," and Leonardo bowed toward the duke. "But even that might not be stretched far enough to protect me from the wrath of the Inquisition if I belittled the sacraments. But I was overcome for a moment by unseemly mirth at the thought of these simple children of nature receiving the rite of baptism. I have read that in many dark and distant places of the earth live savages who have never even heard of the teachings of our faith; yet they are said to have a religion of their own, for God seems to have implanted something of His truth in their hearts. So if they are not ready to accept . . ."

"Leonardo!" cried the duke sharply.

Leonardo da Vinci bit his lip, bowed first to his patron, then to the whispering courtiers, and turned toward the door.

"Stop!" Duke Ludovico commanded so harshly that Mona Cecilia laid a restraining hand on his sleeve. Leonardo turned and waited in proud submission. "I am indeed your friend and stand ready to shield you from the results of your many follies. But I warn you not to go too far. In the future confine your ideas on theology to your notebooks, which, I hear, have grown enormously fat during the last few years."

The cardinal was a man of peace. Now he relaxed in his chair, smoothed his flaming robes, and smiled graciously on the embarrassed company.

"I have grown a little deaf in my left ear," he murmured, "and I call you all to witness it was the left ear I turned toward our young friend as he spoke." His smile faded and an accusing note crept into his smooth tones. "But from what I thought I heard, my son, I was almost ready to believe what I recently heard to your discredit."

Leonardo remained cold and aloof in the doorway.

"Of what am I accused?"

"I refused to believe the charge. How did your detractor put it? Someone remarked in my presence: 'Leonardo da Vinci has become so puffed up with his little learning that he esteems it better to be a philosopher than a Christian.'"

Cecilia cleared the troubled air with her bright laughter. "Some of us hope we may be both," she declared. "Come back and sit here," she invited Leonardo with a nod toward the cushion beside her chair. "Is it true, think you, as one of these same naughty philosophers has told me, that if Columbus explores further into India he will reach the kingdom of Prester John?"

Leonardo, now comfortably relaxed on the cushion of yellow velvet, smiled up into her questioning eyes.

"Sweet lady," he answered, "will you deliver me to the Inquisition as a heretic if I deny that Prester John ever lived, to say nothing of ruling over his kingdom?"

There rose a storm of protest. "We have the proofs . . ." "Marco Polo visited . . ." "At least he affirmed . . ." "Well, Sir John Mandeville has written that he saw with his own eyes . . ."

Leonardo laughed long and heartily. "Sir John Mandeville! What a prince of liars he was! With his own eyes, you say? He had as many eyes as a peacock and, according to his writings, every eye saw wonders that no mortal man ever witnessed before. Snails that cast off shells large enough for a native to dwell in. Two-headed geese! Savages with no heads but providentially provided with eyes in the middle of their stomachs! Though that may easily be accounted for."

The duke who loved oddities of every sort demanded an explanation.

"I have read," Leonardo told him, "that many savages wear gigantic masks in their ceremonial dances to scare away evil spirits. If the English knight saw such a ceremonial dance he might well have mistaken the masks which came to a man's middle for his real head and some gaudy decoration thereon as his eye."

The cardinal would have liked to bring the discussion back to Prester John. Some scholars, he knew, considered that faraway ruler's letter to the pope a forgery; but the pope had answered him, and he decided to avoid a useless argument. So he said instead: "Columbus has reported that in the interior he discovered a tribe of brown men with long tails. Perhaps, Leonardo da Vinci, you can explain these freaks of nature, too."

"Nothing easier! I have read that many monkeys live in those regions. Surely, amid the shadows of the trees, it would be likely that even a careful observer mistook them for naked brown men with tails."

"My philosopher always has his answer," observed the duke

fondly. As Leonardo rose and bent to kiss Cecilia's hand, Ludovico added graciously: "You must not leave before supper."

"I thank you," answered Leonardo, "but the hour is late and I have certain tasks waiting for me in my workshop."

"Let them wait until tomorrow!"

"Tomorrow morning early I have promised to consult with my workmen on building a more practical furnace for the casting of the great horse. If I am permitted to leave . . ."

The duke nodded his dismissal.

Leonardo was glad to escape from the room with its too bright lights and heavy perfumes. For a moment he stood on the threshold of the lofty entrance hall and breathed in gratefully the damp odors of the rose garden he had designed for the Duchess Beatrice. Why had she stayed away from the evening's gathering, he wondered? He glanced toward the still-lighted windows of the apartments he had decorated for her pleasure. If, as the duke had told the company, the lady suffered from migraine, shouldn't she be asleep at this late hour, or, at least, resting in the darkness?

He shrugged impatiently and raised his tired eyes to the stars. Enough of dukes and duchesses, of smirking poets and witch doctors who called themselves physicians. It was good to be alone and to watch the stars.

Another Sea of Darkness, he thought, and every star an island. Another world? If the ingenuity of man might only find a way to cross the mighty, mysterious distance! He thought of the glass he had devised that the moon might seem a little closer. New worlds, perhaps, of which Columbus never dreamed.

Walking through the silent courtyard Leonardo began to dream of a voyage to this strange new world where palm trees waved and rivers rippled over golden sands. He felt a deep and terrible hunger for adventure, for accomplishment. He sat down on a stone bench near the outer gate; suddenly, though he hardly knew why, he began to weep. He was forty years old and tired and he believed that adventure had surely passed him by forever.

Leonardo's ingenious interpretations of travelers' fantasies were borrowed, if that is the proper word, from explanations in "Lands Beyond" by L. Sprague de Camp and Willy Lay, a book which our hero would have thoroughly enjoyed.

Chapter 13

A YEAR after the story of the voyage to India reached Milan, the young duke Gian lay on his deathbed. He did not turn his darkening eyes to his frightened wife who wept beside his pillow; he did not seem to heed the frantic prayers and sobbing of his old nurse who had brought the little Francesco into the death chamber for his father's last, futile blessing. When his confessor had administered the last rites, the youth asked to be left alone. Lonely in his dying, as he had been in his living, Duke Gian passed into the darkness, seeking comfort from his faithful friend, the little hunting hound, stretched out upon the gold-embroidered coverlet.

Never had Gian's uncle, Duke Ludovico, played the fox so convincingly. When the young duke's garishly decked body was brought from the palace at Pavia to lie in state in the cathedral of Milan, Duke Ludovico seemed to lose all self-control. As he stood beside the corpse, he broke down altogether. In a grief-choked voice he swore to be a guardian to Gian's little son, heir to the dukedom of Milan and the rich lands of Lombardy.

Ludovico had been granted sufficient opportunity to perfect his plotting during the months Duke Gian lay suffering in his death chamber. Of course, he now showed surprised horror when even the late duke's supporters cried out that a regency which would extend over a decade might prove disastrous to Milan. If the treacherous Venetians or the greedy French, these gentlemen argued, once realized the weakness of the Milanese government, nominally headed by so young a child, invasion and all the horrors of war would smite the country. Better one strong ruler, they suggested, than a council of advisors who would weaken their power by endless quarreling among themselves.

Meanwhile the commoners, less subtle but just as certain of their desires as the governing nobles, took matters into their own hands. The lawful ruler of Milan had long been pushed into the background; Ludovico had already been accepted as their rightful duke by the populace who loved him for his seemingly bluff good-nature and his many lavish spectacles. The first time that Ludovico appeared in public after his nephew's burial, thousands of voices greeted him as the Duke of Milan and the ruler over Lombardy.

The councilors decided that the voice of the people was for once the voice of God and begged Il Moro to depose the child ruler. Isabella of Aragona tragically beautiful in her widow's weeds, tried in vain to rally support for her son. But the few who remained faithful to Gian's memory had not the stomachs to risk death or exile for little Francesco. Soon Duchess Isabella suffered banishment, made more bitter by her fears for her little son. He remained in Il Moro's hands "to insure his safety."

For the first time since her marriage Beatrice d'Este felt secure in her position. Gian was dead; Isabella, the little duchess's proud rival, had suffered utter and shameful defeat and could not hope that her son would ever rule Milan. Beatrice was confident that some day her own beloved Maximiliano would become his father's heir; she had had the child christened Ercole but believed it a good omen to change his name to that of the great ruler whose glory he might some day emulate. And now that she expected to bear her husband another child, thus making Ludovico's dynastic rights more secure, there was something like peace and loving understanding between the ill-mated couple.

The little lady expressed her new-found happiness by a bout of frivolity and gaiety which startled even the pleasure-loving Milanese court. Leonardo da Vinci must design a really startling ball gown for the fete she planned to commemorate her wedding anniversary. She had already ordered Bellincioni to write a masque; costumes and stage settings must be ready, and it was all nonsense that the duke desired Leonardo to spend every possible moment on the completion of the great horse!

The halls of the castle those raw December nights were bright with firelight and the flame of torches. Feast followed feast. After the guests had gorged themselves on roast peacocks and pastries and ices fashioned in curious shapes of beast or flower, they staggered from the disordered tables to listen to music, or to sit in a merry circle and exchange tales and riddles. Or there might be cards, a diversion both the duke and duchess dearly loved, for, strange to say, they were always successful at the gaming table.

But always when the cathedral chimes assured the yawning guests that it was midnight, those who longed for permission to seek their beds were disappointed. Beatrice would spring from her chair, toss her long, beribboned braid over her shoulders, and call to the musicians to begin a dance tune. Leonardo da Vinci as he watched her whirl past him and heard her wild laughter above the music thought more than once of a curious story he had lately read: how a beautiful girl incurred the envy of a witch who in revenge caused the damsel to dance without ceasing to her early grave.

On a night of sparkling frost, which reminded many of the January weather that had welcomed Ludovico's bride to Milan, the music sickened into silence and the dancing stopped.

Beneath the richly embroidered coverings of her bed the Duchess Beatrice writhed in agony. Her shrill screaming echoed through the halls so lately filled with light and love and laughter. Ambrogio with several physicians of higher repute, the court astrologers, and the withered midwives jostled one another in their zeal to ease their mistress. In growing despair Duke Ludovico watched several hastily summoned monks display holy relics before his wife's unseeing eyes. He turned away to grope for comfort from Beatrice's favorite dwarf, deformed and bitter-tongued, who had learned to love her.

Beneath the high, ornate ceilings of the bedchamber, the chanting of the prayers for the dying rose; the sonorous Latin phrases drowned the wailing of the weeping attendants. It was not until the first wintry sunlight struggled to pierce the heavy curtains that Duchess Beatrice d'Este followed her new-born child into silence.

To Duke Ludovico in his first noisy grief it seemed that no sorrow which had ever afflicted mortal man could be compared to his sorrow. He turned from all the pleasures of the flesh; "as though determined to keep an early Lent!" exclaimed one awed courtier. He even refused to eat his meager meals at an ordinary table but insisted that a servant serve him on a bare board as he sat, unkempt and unshaven, in a darkened room. Not even the beautifully phrased condolences of Cardinal Ippolito d'Este could comfort him.

But soon the duke found a little consolation in discussing with his favorite artist a fitting memorial for his loved, lost lady. He ordered Leonardo to be summoned from his labors on the equestrian statue.

Leonardo da Vinci had grown weary of the project that he had begun so long ago with such high hopes. He agreed with his critics that his first plan was far too ambitious and costly. A wagon large and strong enough to bear the weight of the mighty horse and its rider had transported it to the courtyard of Ludovico's castle.

Every day Leonardo went to view his creation with critically objective eyes. Perhaps the slightest change here, he decided, or a bit of alteration there, might improve it. Il Moro seemed pleased but made no definite promise that soon the monument would be immortalized in metal. He added impressively that surely Leonardo as a military expert must realize how uncertain the times were with the growing threat of French invasion. Even if sufficient metal could be obtained, which the duke doubted, since the states to which he might apply were preparing for war, such metal should

be hoarded by Milan for cannons not statues. But, of course—
Ludovico ended the conference—he was delighted with the model
for the memorial to his illustrious father.

At this time Leonardo's own enthusiasm had been considerably
dampened by the duke's laxity in money matters. That extravagant
gentleman seemed to forget that the Florentine could hardly be
expected to pay his workmen and support his household on the
fifty ducats Il Moro had been induced to hand over to him within
the space of three years.

The duke, blithely oblivious of his obligations, had been greatly
surprised when Leonardo actually refused to finish decorating certain apartments in the *castello* on the plea that he must spend his
time on more profitable work. It was during this harassed period
that Leonardo devoted much of his energy to such practical inventions as a machine for sharpening needles and a spinner which
would have revolutionized Milan's chief industry, could he have
found someone with enough imagination to try it. But these ideas
brought him no money and the plans remained buried in his notebooks.

Il Moro, who had been greatly annoyed by Leonardo's demands
for his salary, graciously forgave him and as a mark of his renewed
favor offered the artist a new commission. Duke Moro explained
that he wished the room, in which he intended to mourn his lost
lady for his remaining years, to be turned into a fitting memorial
to the dead duchess.

But before the dark and gloomy decorations were half finished
the sorrowing husband decided it would be better for the Florentine
to devote his genius to decorating the adjacent banquet hall. Duke
Ludovico could think of no better way to commemorate the great
joy which had come to supplant his grief for Beatrice. A kindly
Providence, to relieve his sorrow, had permitted Lucrezia to bear
him a son. Moro decided that he would celebrate the happy event
by emerging from his retirement to feast and make merry in the
newly decorated banquet hall.

Unfortunately for the duke's plans, Leonardo da Vinci, as so many
times before, became so engrossed in his creation that it seemed he

would never complete it. He became fascinated by the idea of turning the hall into a bower built of fantastic branches. He contrived an elaborate combination of leaves and plaited twigs; the design, although wildly imaginative, suggested the discipline of the mathematician who thought in squares and circles and the botanist who had closely observed the growing plants he now reproduced in exaggerated forms. Leonardo lingered so long over his startling designs that his work on the banquet hall was not completed until the spring of 1498.

Il Moro was pleased when his guests shrieked their praises of the newly decorated hall, but the unfortunate man carried a new sorrow in his heart. When Leonardo had forced him to delay the banquet to mark the birth of Lucrezia's son, the duke had secretly decided it might be more seemly to mark the completion of the hall with a wedding celebration. For by this time Il Moro knew he was madly in love with a lively young widow, the sister-in-law of Isabella d'Este. The lady had rather a rowdy reputation even for those liberal days, but Ludovico was inclined to overlook her former follies. For her late husband had been a French count with influential relatives. Since Duke Ludovico had reason to fear the French he thought it wise to strengthen his connections with the French court.

The lady was willing but the French king, who decided that Ludovico's character was no better than his prospective bride's, decided to prevent further scandal and forbade the marriage.

Although he felt that he suffered a second bereavement, the widower enjoyed the banquet and heartily echoed his guests' praises of Leonardo's handicraft. Leonardo's patron actually showed his appreciation by rewarding his court painter a year later with a vineyard sixteen rods long. The duke made the gracious suggestion that Leonardo should build a house on his new property to cement the bonds which already existed between them.

Leonardo took great pride in his new possession. He was an artist, recklessly generous to his associates and often impractical. But he carried somewhere in his make-up the shrewd business sense of generations of successful notaries. Like a true da Vinci he re-

joiced that for the first time in all his laborious life he owned a plot
of land and might some day live on it in a house of his own.

Both patron and court painter would have been shocked to learn
how soon the colorful, extravagant life in Milan would end. At
the banquet table Il Moro sat surrounded by his flattering courtiers
and drank himself into a state of blissful security. Leonardo was
not present to feel disgust at the slobbering mouth and drunken
laughter. He had with difficulty persuaded his patron to grant him
permission to spend the evening in his own workshop.

A friend from Florence dropped in and shared Leonardo's frugal
supper, which otherwise would have been a solitary meal. For the
master instead of eating with his apprentices had refused to break
off his examination of the bag of shells that now stood half-empty
on the littered table. Early that morning several peasants, who had
heard something of the court painter's peculiar interests, had
brought him a bag of shells and coral.

Leonardo had paid the men generously for the stones they said
they had gathered in the mountains near Parma. Again, as in his
boyhood days, he wondered what miracle had brought these sea-
bred creatures to rest so far inland. A miracle, yes, but not the
miracle of Noah's flood as Leonardo's old teacher had insisted. That
explanation was as far-fetched, he felt, as the conclusion of those
who insisted that the all-powerful stars caused the formation of
fossils. If only he could bring forth reasonable proof!

Now over a cup of thin wine he forced himself to listen to his
friend's account of the latest happenings in Florence.

"You have surely heard of Savonarola?"

"Yes, yes," answered Leonardo absently, for one part of his brain
still continued to mull over the problem he had set himself. "The
mad prior who since the death of his protector, Lorenzo de' Medici,
has urged Florence to accept no earthly ruler but to acknowledge
Christ as king."

"You do right to call him mad although he is a holy man. And
now his latest folly: the Bonfire of Vanities."

Leonardo forced himself to show a little interest in his visitor's
report.

"What 'Vanities'?" he asked.

"Perhaps," conceded the Florentine, "he is right to preach that Florence will be punished for its sins unless it renounces its vices. He organized an army of young people, many of them little more than children, to spy upon the failings of their elders and to report them to the authorities. Also to collect all sinful frivolities to be publicly burned in the piazza."

His voice rose shrill with indignation: "Not 'Vanities' alone, like carnival masks and rougepots and the broidered ribbons he has forbidden Florentine women to wear. No, last week he and his followers condemned to the flames precious scrolls, only because they were covered with the writings of heathen philosophers. And at the same time they destroyed confiscated statues and pictures of great merit merely because they portrayed the gods of the Greeks and Romans."

He hesitated a moment. "How can I tell you? But you will surely learn the truth and it is best you hear it first from a friend. The canvas you painted when a pupil in Verrocchio's studio—the naked goddess . . . !" His grief and anger choked off further speech.

Leonardo da Vinci was neither grieved nor angered. It seemed to him at that moment that another man had limned the loveliness now perished in the flames. He had painted so many other pictures; he would paint many more. Just now he wanted to be left in peace to study his fossils. But, always the gentleman, Leonardo leaned across the table and sought to comfort his outraged friend.

Chapter 14

*I*T MEANT much to Leonardo da Vinci to be permitted to continue in Milan the anatomical studies he had begun in Florence. Verrocchio, Leonardo's master, had never failed to urge upon his pupils the necessity of studying the structure of the human body. But since few of his own works portrayed the nude figure, Verrocchio's anatomical studies were somewhat superficial. As in so many other fields, the student soon surpassed the master.

Leonardo had become interested in anatomy as an artist; as always, his first investigations lured him further and further and the scientist began to search beneath the surface and to draw deductions from all that he had discovered.

Artists who made a serious study of anatomy were no rarity in the Italy of Leonardo's day. For one thing they were closely allied to physicians. Painters bought their pigments at the apothecary shops and became acquainted with the owners who had absorbed an empirical and often fantastic knowledge of drugs and healing. Many patients survived their loathsome brews of snakefat and bats' liver and mandrake root—a remarkable testimony to the powers of resistance in the human body. In these shops an artist often lingered to chat with one of the few physicians who purchased rather than concocted his own drugs. There was always a cordial relationship between artists and doctors during Leonardo's youth in Florence for both groups belonged to the same guild which had for its patron Saint Luke, painter and physician.

There was a much more cogent reason, Leonardo soon discovered, for cultivating the friendship of prominent physicians. He had long despised the breed; in his notebooks he suggested it was far safer for a man to prevent illness by careful diet and sensible habits than to trust an ignorant, mercenary bungler who would profit from his patient's misery. Since the art of anatomical illustration was still in its infancy, Leonardo had little opportunity to study medical charts and drawings. He had long ago satisfied his scientific curiosity by dissecting various animals. But only a prominent physician was officially permitted to dissect a human body.

For a long time both church and state official frowned upon human dissections, even when they were performed by teachers of anatomy. A natural revulsion against the practice made it almost impossible to secure for this purpose cadavers even of executed criminals. But during Leonardo's apprentice days in Florence, a prominent professor of anatomy at the nearby University of Pisa occasionally performed an anatomy to which not only medical students but all who might be interested were permitted to attend.

Years later in Milan Leonardo da Vinci again felt the urge to continue his anatomical studies. His illustrations for the mathematical works of Fra Luca Pacioli reawakened Leonardo's interest in proportion, "not only in numbers and measures," he writes, but in the human body. Now in the lengthening May twilight he bent over his drawing board, eager to finish his latest anatomical study that he might show it to Pacioli whom he expected later that evening. Leonardo frowned when Giacomo, whistling a rowdy streetsong, entered the studio.

Salai, as the master now called his protégé, had changed from a cherubic-faced child to a slender, handsome youth whom Leonardo delighted to paint. One of these portraits in red chalk showed the lad in his sixteenth year, the classical beauty of his profile heightened by his tumbled curls. But only his beauty gave Leonardo pleasure for the boy was still greedy and insolent and consistently ungrateful for all the favors showered upon him. At first he seemed to show a bent for painting but Leonardo, in spite of all his fondness for Salai, knew he would never rise above mediocrity.

"I told you at supper I did not wish to be disturbed," rebuked Leonardo.

As though to explain the interruption, Salai held out the handsomely tooled leather purse that swung from his girdle; it was empty.

Still frowning, Leonardo went to his strongbox and counted out a handful of small coins. Salai grunted his thanks and, resuming his song, swung through the curtained doorway. Leonardo knew better than to ask where he intended to spend the evening. Why encourage Salai to lie to him? The master sighed but forgot his irritation as he bent over his drawing board.

Fra Pacioli looked up from the sketches to praise them enthusiastically. "This drawing of the muscles!" he exclaimed. "It is not anatomy; why, 'tis art."

"You forget," Leonardo modestly reminded the Franciscan, "that as an anatomist, I am a mere amateur."

Fra Luca stubbornly shook his head. "Then you are an amateur whose work surpasses that of many masters," he insisted. "Ah, but what confusion!" He pointed to the corner of the sheet which was covered with sketches intermingled with Leonardo's reversed script. "Here you draw the muscles of the leg. And beside it a tomb which one of the early Etruscan princes might have built. And here . . . But what part of the human system are you studying now?"

"So little has been written on the nervous system," answered Leonardo, "that I hope to make a complete study of the nerves of every part of the body. Not only the cause of nerve sicknesses like paralysis and epilepsy but the nerves connected with sleep and hunger and the nerves that govern our lips when we speak or smile."

"If you could only publish this material!" said Fra Pacioli. "It would be of the greatest value."

"I hope to some day, at least my ideas on painting and my anatomical studies if I ever have time to complete them. But I have just begun. There are so many other notes that should be collected and revised—on botany, geology, astronomy." He leaned over to smile into his friend's eyes; now he spoke almost in a whisper. "Do you know what I scrawled in a margin last month after our talk of Ptolemy and his study of the heavenly bodies? I set down my belief: The sun does not move."

Fra Luca's eyes turned swiftly toward the curtained door.

"We are safe," Leonardo da Vinci assured his guest. "The pupils who share my quarters are off to some merrymaking; the servants are gone, too. I am not always as indiscreet as I was that evening when I read the letter of Christopher Columbus. Remember?"

The monk nodded. "You stand high in the duke's favor and if you should ever need his protection—but we are warned, 'put not your faith in princes,'" he ended with a cynical smile. "But you reminded me when you mentioned Columbus of a letter I received this very morning; 'tis from my nephew who is a member of the Roman College. I brought it for you to read." He fumbled in the folds of his woolen habit. "Ah, here is the copy my nephew sent me. Read for yourself what he says of the latest reports that have reached Rome of our explorer."

The monk turned back to the worktable to re-examine several sketches that had intrigued him. Leonardo leaned back his chair and began to read the Jesuit scholar's delicate script. "The fellow is mad!" he exclaimed.

"You mean my nephew?" demanded Fra Pacioli in pretended offense; but his eyes twinkled.

"No, for he is reasonable enough to wonder how a man of Columbus' skill and daring could write such arrant nonsense as appears in his *Book of Prophecies.*"

"But my nephew, who has read it, says that the Prophecies are based on Holy Writ," murmured the monk.

"Yes, but the fool quotes also from one Esdras whom he seems to consider a true prophet. Here," Leonardo choked with rage, "he dares to say that this same prophet directed him more truly than the maps of Toscanelli. He insists that the Hebrew Isaiah was his pilot across the Sea of Darkness."

"You have left much of the matter unread," Pacioli reminded him dryly.

"And here," Leonardo burst out a moment later, "here your nephew quotes from a letter our navigator penned on his third voyage. So he has discovered a river that he believes is the Ganges and must therefore flow from Paradise! And he goes on: 'I think that Paradise is in a place that nobody can reach except by divine will. It has the form of a rough mountain and it resembles the end of a pear; little by little, approaching there from afar one mounts slowly towards it. These are great indications of the Earthly Paradise, because the site conforms to the opinion of holy and wise theologians.' "

Thoroughly exasperated, Leonardo da Vinci flung the letter upon the worktable.

"You have not finished my nephew's report," teased Fra Luca. "Never mind, it is only some nonsense about using the gold mines and spicery of India to fight a new war for the Holy Sepulcher which Columbus believes can be recaptured for Christendom in the space of three years. Which," the Franciscan ended laughingly, "makes our discoverer not only a navigator and theologian but something of a military expert."

But Leonardo refused to share his friend's mirth.

"I see nothing amusing in the fact," he said bitterly, "that such honor should be paid to one who credits his discoveries to Isaiah rather than Toscanelli. Why should a mathematician toil for years to leave calculations to guide an ungrateful fool?"

Fra Luca's merry eyes grew suddenly grave. "Toscanelli did not draw his maps for the sake of an ignorant sailor," he answered, "any more than you painted your 'Last Supper' for the pleasure of the scatter-brained sensualist, Il Moro."

Leonardo's bitter face softened.

"You are right," he said softly. "Toscanelli served his science when he made his calculations as I worship Our Lady when I paint her and her little son." He hesitated, then rapidly began to turn the sheets he had taken from a secret drawer of his worktable. "I know I can trust you. It is somewhat daring, but you will not betray me. And only a mathematician like you can understand."

He lay before the monk a page covered with sketches of various machines under which appeared notations and figures. His finger pointed to a small drawing crowded and almost lost among the other sketches.

It was a drawing of Mary and the young Jesus. "The Flight into Egypt!" said Fra Luca, for the two figures seemed to be surrounded by a desolate desert. He peered closer that he might discern what the mother, who sat upon a stone, drew in the sand at her feet. Yes, she drew triangles and circles as though instructing the child beside her.

"My old teacher Verrocchio believed that geometry was the source of all our knowledge," said Leonardo softly.

"I thank you for letting me see your sketch which you must never complete," murmured the mathematician much moved.

He did not speak again until Leonardo carefully hid the sheet between the others and stowed the bundle in the drawer of his worktable. Then: "I wondered to see you so wroth over the follies of that simple discoverer. True, he is a dreamer of dreams. Perhaps only by dreams could he find his way across the Sea of Darkness. And you, my dear Leonardo, should be the last one to chide a man for his visions."

"Do you accuse me of being a dreamer?" Leonardo spoke rather stiffly for he prided himself on being the most practical of men.

"For one who tries to govern his life by reason you sometimes show yourself as visionary as . . . as that misguided Dominican, Savonarola," answered the monk, and he crossed himself as he spoke. "He, too, followed his dreams although they led him to the gallows. I sickened yesterday when a traveler from Florence told me how he died, but . . ."

"And now you compare me to . . . ?

"Your dream is very different, Leonardo, but still I fear for you. I have heard—what man in Milan has not heard?—of the machines you have made and destroyed, still seeking to perfect the miracle which will bear you above the earth."

Leonardo's eyes turned toward a carefully covered object in a corner of the long room.

"Why call me mad or my hope to fly a dream?" he asked. "Was Roger Bacon, a Franciscan like you, a dreamer or mad? Two hundred years ago this genius in optics, this astronomer and philosopher, said that the air was a limited body, like the sea. Some day man would be able to float on top of the air, he believed, as easily as he now floats upon the water."

"But what plans did he leave? What sketches—such as you are always drawing?" asked Fra Luca, nodding toward the piled-up notebooks.

"I have never heard of any," answered Leonardo sadly. "But if the illustrious Roger Bacon believed . . ."

The monk laughed long and heartily. "Illustrious, yes. But still a little mad. Do you know his prophecy that someday chariots would move—and move faster—through mechanical power than if drawn by horses?"

"Perhaps," said Leonardo da Vinci bitingly, "perhaps you will report my madness to Ambrogio, the court physician. And since he hates me because I have sneered at his astrology, he will be most happy to have me whipped and kept in chains for my lunacy. But first," and he rose and pointed a menacing finger at his friend, "but first, let me assure you there is every reason why Roger Bacon's prophecy of a horseless chariot should come to pass. I have already devised a model of such a chariot; it is fitted with a steering bar and transmission gear."

Fra Pacioli gasped.

"But does it really move?" he demanded, breathlessly.

Leonardo sadly shook his head. "Only a few yards. But when I have perfected the mechanism . . . Ah, my friend, I sometimes think I shall not live long enough to complete even a third of the many devices I have commenced."

Chapter 15

*I*N APRIL, in the year 1500, Leonardo da Vinci set down in his notebook: "The duke has lost his kingdom, his possessions, his liberty, and all his works have come to nought."

This was his epitaph for the man under whose patronage Leonardo had spent sixteen secure and productive years. Later he learned of the ending of the drama of ambition and intrigue which had been Duke Ludovico's life. The former ruler played the final tragic act in an underground dungeon, where he scratched crude, childish drawings on the damp walls and scrawled brave, sententious sayings to strengthen his broken spirit. After eight years he died, still a prisoner of the French king.

Leonardo who wrote of many things never penned a single line of pity for the duke's sufferings. He was not insensitive to the prisoner's misery. No one could have recognized more keenly the irony of Il Moro's fate: his regal raiment of red and white rotting to filthy rags which hardly covered his shivering nakedness; after the lofty, bright halls of the *castello* at Milan, bright with torches and sweet with perfume, the dank darkness of a dungeon cell; no music now, no sound of lutes and laughter, only the drip, drip of water down the blackened walls.

Yet for all the vividness of the picture his fancy drew, Leonardo felt hardly a pang of pity for the deposed duke. Once in the woods near Vinci he had watched a snake engulf the jeweled brightness of a humming bird. He had felt no pity, only curiosity that such cruelty could exist in a beautiful universe. Now sympathy gave way to a greater wonder at man's inhumanity to his fellow-man. Leonardo had viewed with the same impersonal detachment the upheaval and the bloodshed which had led to his duke's downfall.

Italy with its fabled wealth had long been a temptation to French kings and German emperors. For over a thousand years Italy had been broken up into a number of city-states. Constantly at war with each other, these states were often ready to call on foreign rulers to help them win their battles.

While Duke Gian still lived, Ludovico had induced Charles VIII, king of France, to take a hand in Milanese politics. Charles, who was as feeble of will as he was puny of body, was easily seduced by Ludovico's flattery and the charm of Duchess Beatrice; he promised his royal protection to the scheming pair. Unfortunately for Milan and Duke Ludovico, who shortly afterwards usurped the ruling power, Charles' death brought about the accession of Louis XII.

Louis XII was eager for Italian territory and war loot; he needed only the slightest pretext for invasion. He disliked Duke Ludovico; he knew also that Milan, girded by rich farmlands, would prove an ideal breadbasket for his famished soldiers.

The French soldiers, as greedy though not as ruthless as the hordes of Genghis Khan, pillaged the lovely city. Soon the archers discovered the colossus of Leonardo da Vinci. The heroic equestrian statue had never been cast in bronze; now the clay model loomed unprotected in a courtyard of Ludovico's castle. A tempting target! The archers fitted their arrows and took careful aim. In a few moments the horse and rider, the still unfinished masterpiece over which Leonardo had toiled so many years, became a thing of horror, marred and dishonored by the enemy's brutal sport. After a few months of wind and weather nothing remained of Leonardo's memorial to the founder of the house of Sforza but lumps of undistinguished clay.

Leonardo felt that life in Milan without his former patron would become untenable. With uncharacteristic shrewdness he sent his savings to a Florentine bank for safe-keeping. Accompanied by Luca Pacioli and young Salai, Leonardo da Vinci left the city to accept a long-standing invitation to visit Isabella d'Este, wife of the ruler of Mantua.

Isabella d'Este was a lover of the New Learning, the patron of poets and artists and musicians. Her sister Beatrice, of unhappy memory, had madly pursued the deer and the wild boar in the woods about Milan; Isabella was a huntress, too, but she attempted to capture only lions.

As Leonardo's fame increased the lady's urgency increased also. Leonardo, she had written, must ask Duke Ludovico's permission to visit the court of Mantua; he must add one of his masterpieces to the many which already adorned her castle. Perhaps he would paint her portrait? Maybe he had heard that she sang a little and played the lute, she added modestly; it would mean much if he contributed his musical gifts to her nightly concerts.

Now at the home of Isabella d'Este, in whose court gathered the most gifted Italians of his day, Leonardo enjoyed for a little while the company of his peers, good talk and music. Not the least of his happiness was due to his renewed fellowship with his old friend, Atalante Miglioretti, the lute-player whom the music-loving lady had lured from Milan. Atalante was quieter and graver than Leonardo remembered him—as became the father of an adored child to whom Isabella had consented to act as godmother. Gone were his madcap pranks, his youthful enthusiasms. Polished and urbane, he had become the perfect courtier.

Atalante warned his friend of perhaps the greatest of Isabella's failings. "She collects poets and musicians and artists as determinedly as she collects rare books and sculpture," he said. "And to all of them, even the most accomplished, she would be not only the friend but the teacher." He laughed a little shamefacedly. "The lady has a voice of rare quality and has studied under excellent teachers. Perhaps that is why when I play an accompaniment for her singing she chides me for a false note as she might scold her baby son Federigo for some childish fault."

Leonardo did not seem to listen. He had stooped to pluck an unfamiliar flower as they walked through the lovely gardens, now heavy with the twilight dew. It might be a windflower, he thought, but no, what would such a wilding be doing in the prim, carefully tended borders?

"It is the same with you gentlemen of the brush and pencil," went on the lute-player. "I am disclosing no secret for this is common gossip in Mantua. When our lady commissions an artist, even one of great repute like Andrea Mantegna, to decorate her walls, she dictates full directions to one of her secretaries. More, with the sketch the artist receives exact measurements for his picture and a tape measure, lest he fall into error."

"Why do you tell me all this?"

"Because I know that Isabella d'Este has long pleaded with you to do her portrait and . . ."

"You forget," said Leonardo coldly, "that I am not Andrea Mantegna but Leonardo da Vinci."

The artist's pride overawed even Isabella when she ventured to suggest a picture she desired him to paint for her.

"If you will accept the idea . . . Naturally, I do not suggest the treatment which I know will be worthy," she assured Leonardo with unusual humility. "And I promise not to be too impatient if it is late in delivery."

Leonardo da Vinci, politely reserved, refused to discuss the proposed painting. Ever since Isabella had marveled at the artist's first portrait of Cecilia Gallerani, she had been determined to sit for the Milanese court painter. Now he finally consented and began a sketch of his hostess. But he never tried to find time to do the painting for which the sketch was a preliminary study. Again and again Isabella d'Este wrote her favorite artist and pleaded for the promised portrait. At last Leonardo ended the matter by answering her with unusual rudeness. For a while the disappointed lady treasured a copy of the sketch which the artist had negligently thrown aside. But Gonzaga, Isabella's husband, was repelled by the feeling of cold dislike which the artist had allowed to creep into the drawing. Isabella greatly grieved when, without her knowledge and consent, Gonzaga presented the sketch to another admirer of the stubborn painter.

From Mantua Leonardo da Vinci traveled to Venice. At any other time the city which ruled the Adriatic like a queen, languorous and opulent, would have dazzled him with her beauty. Even now, with the air heavy with the excitement of war and threatened invasion, Leonardo grew so bemused with his first glimpse of the domes of St. Marks and its furiously plunging bronze horses that he stood openmouthed beside the Grand Canal and allowed the fawning gondolier to charge him double.

He had escaped from the too fervent hospitality of Isabella d'Este by hinting that secret affairs of state called him to Venice. Although this was an expedient excuse it should not be called a brazen falsehood. Leonardo had grown weary of poetry and allegorical murals, of lute-playing and Latin comedies. He had heard rumors that Venice lay at the mercy of the unmerciful Turks. Leonardo decided that the poorly fortified city of palaces might prove most congenial to a restless military engineer in search of employment.

His services were so desperately needed in Venice that for once the military experts did not refuse to consider the ideas of a man who was not only an amateur in their profession but under suspicion as a foreigner. After a hasty study of the terrain, Leonardo informed the Venetian authorities that the hinterland might be protected from Turkish invaders by even a scanty force. He also worked as a gunmaker and recorded his experiences in a statement irritating in its brevity: "Bombards . . . at Venice."

But the entries he set down in his notebook in 1501 were not always so laconic. Leonardo hoped to gain a victory for the Venetians by several startling inventions he recorded with great care in his secret script, inventions he described only in part to the desperate authorities. The idea of a diving suit was not original with the Florentine. Under his sketch of a diver's equipment he gave a full description of a garment worn by pearl divers in the Indian Ocean. But the improved suit Leonardo devised in Venice was so constructed that the air supplied the diver would, the inventor hoped, last four hours. This would enable the wearer to swim a long distance under water and approach the enemy's fleet unobserved.

Even more sensational were Leonardo's sketch and description of what he elsewhere called "a ship to be used to sink another ship." Here he grew so secretive that he did not depend alone on his usual mirror-writing but left incomplete some of his directions for using the new and dreadful weapon. He was so confident of the success of his scheme that he added the suggestion that the Venetians, who watched from the shore, should provide themselves with chains to bind the captured Turks as they swam to land.

These notes of Leonardo da Vinci have been preserved; we know that he actually was in contact with the terrified Venetian government. But there is no other record of what must have been the most exciting episode of all his forty-eight years. We know only that no weapon by Leonardo da Vinci was employed against the Turks. Did he ever complete the diving suit or the submarine, only to watch them prove untrustworthy and useless? Or did he for the first time realize the horror he would bring upon the world if what had hitherto seemed a madman's dream became reality? Did he keep silent before the Venetian authorities because as he was to say years afterwards:

> How and why I do not describe my method of remaining under water . . . I do not publish or divulge . . . by reason of the evil nature of men, who would use [it] as means of murder at the bottom of the sea, by breaking the bottom of ships and sinking them together with the men in them.

Is this the answer to the enigma of the Venetian adventure? Or must it still remain a mystery as baffling as the smile of the lady whose picture Leonardo was soon to paint in Florence?

Chapter 16

ON EASTER Sunday, 1501, the worshipers at the Church of
the Annunciation in Florence crowded before a new picture, a preliminary study of the Virgin Mary, her child and her mother, Saint
Anne. Artists marveled at the perfect balance of the strangely
disposed figures, for who had ever imagined it would be possible
to seat Mary on her mother's lap without a touch of the grotesque,
or at least a loss of dignity? The common folk cried aloud in their
admiration of the sweetness and gravity of the two women, the
appealing roguishness of Mary's child.

But many grew disturbed at the smile of Saint Anne. For it was
at once aloof yet compassionate and haunting in its mystery. Those
who knew Leonardo da Vinci, who shortly after his return to
Florence had been commissioned to paint this picture for the
Church of the Annunciation, remarked that they had sometimes
seen the artist wear that same smile of tender playfulness.

Now that "The Cartoon for the Madonna and Child with
St. Anne" was completed and universally praised, Leonardo grew
indifferent about completing the picture. A visitor to Florence
reported he had found the artist so deeply engaged in his mathe-

matical studies that he seemed to shrink from taking up his paint-brushes. The Servite monks, who had commissioned the painting, began to grumble over the large sums they had advanced Leonardo for the support of his household which included several young artists as well as Andrea Salai. But when could duke or priest or patron ever hurry Leonardo da Vinci!

Now into the quiet of Leonardo da Vinci's life flashed a glittering figure whom some called the Antichrist because of his crimes, and others hailed as the savior of all Italy.

It could hardly have been discretion which kept Leonardo from recording among his other secrets his private estimate of Cesare Borgia. Rather he seems to have withheld judgment or to have had little interest in the whirlpool of intrigue and violence which eddied about him.

Leonardo knew that Cesare, with the ruthlessness of a naked savage, tortured and killed the enemies he had snared with his treachery. But why condemn the cat with the bleeding mouse, the spider as it approaches the tangled fly? Leonardo might have decided that his new friend, the Florentine state secretary, Niccolo Machiavelli, judged wisely. And Machiavelli, a shrewd politician, believed that Cesare Borgia held the hope of the future in his strong, sure hands. "Florence may some day be a great state," Machiavelli told Leonardo, "and a truly great state needs a truly great—and ruthless!—prince to govern it."

A man far more clear-sighted than Leonardo da Vinci might have been convinced by Machiavelli, who spoke and wrote with the seeming ease with which Leonardo painted. The secretary described to his friend a more secure and peaceful society in a united Italy, an idea which seemed then as fantastic as Leonardo's own secret dreams of a new heaven and a new earth. But while Machiavelli plotted practical measures, Leonardo could only dream. Machiavelli told his new friend that it was foolish for an artist and inventor and engineer to clutter his head with political opinions.

Leonardo knew that the graceful, flaxen-haired warrior betrayed the women who loved him, the allies who trusted him, as lightly as he had abandoned forever his cardinal's robes for a coat of mail. There were rumors of crimes and vices no decent citizen could repeat without flinching. Yet when Leonardo da Vinci came to meet this man of deeds as black as the velvet mask he so often wore, he too fell a victim to the Borgia's magnetic charm.

For some hectic months Leonardo put his talents at the service of this dictator who boasted that he would eat up city-state after city-state in Italy as a man nibbles leaf after leaf of an artichoke. Under the title of Architect and Engineer General, Leonardo traveled from town to town in the ever-widening territory that had fallen under Borgia's control. He built canals and fortifications, drained swamps, surveyed, and made military maps, each a work of art, with clearly defined roads, down one of which Borgia planned his soldiers would march to attack Florence.

Leonardo soon left the service of the adventurer whom Machiavelli chose for the hero of his political masterpiece, *The Prince*. Long before Cesare Borgia had stumbled down the path of treachery and murder to suffer an exile's death at the end, Leonardo returned to Florence. Here in the autumn of 1503 he rejoined the guild of Florentine artists, gathered a number of young painters about him, and with undiminished vigor began certain ambitious projects both in the field of engineering and art.

Chapter 17

*I*T WAS a time of shifting loyalties. A soldier might sell his sword, an engineer his skills, to the highest bidder. Leonardo da Vinci's service to Cesare Borgia did not cause him to lose favor with the Florentine authorities. On the contrary, they esteemed him the more for having gained the confidence of an enemy so learned in the art of warfare.

Now that Florence had renewed its war against its old rival, Pisa, Leonardo's grandiose plan of stripping the enemy of its power appealed to the city fathers. He proposed to use the Arno for his weapon and explained how the river might be turned from its bed into two canals. The water thus directed would flow into the sea at Leghorn; Pisa, at that time a flourishing seaport town, would be deprived of its access to the sea.

Accompanied by a civil servant who knew something of engineering, Leonardo set out for the Florentine headquarters near Pisa. Here the military authorities eagerly accepted his proposal and urged that it be carried out as soon as possible, both for the protection of their own troops and the embarrassment of the enemy.

On returning to Florence, Leonardo first worked feverishly on

114

a map that showed the water courses of Tuscany, their tributaries and lakes. Then he sketched the mechanized devices necessary to carry out his project. He described, both by picture and written word, the various appliances needed to lift stones out of the canal bed and to level the ground with the minimum of time and physical effort. By his knowledge of the minutest details Leonardo indicated how thoroughly the dreamer of dreams had become submerged in the practical man of action.

But Leonardo's efforts were delayed by the constant bickerings of the commanding officers, who soon expressed their resentment toward the unwelcomed civilian. Machiavelli brought about something like peace and the work continued. Then the collapse of Cesare Borgia's power filled the Florentines with a new sense of security. It might not be necessary after all to destroy the prosperity of Pisa!

Leonardo da Vinci agreed. He seemed pleased to turn from war measures to proposals more suitable for an era of peace. He reminded certain Florentine statesmen that Lorenzo de' Medici had discussed the building of a canal from Prato to Signa. But now he, Leonardo, outlined his plans for a waterway larger and more useful than anyone had yet conceived. He urged the various guilds to help carry out his scheme since many industries would profit through the building of the canal.

The sketches for the great canal and the detailed descriptions which explained them were slipped between the covers of certain notebooks to remain buried for many sterile years. Leonardo suddenly discovered that he needed money. He had received no salary since leaving the employ of Cesare Borgia. While planning for the canal Leonardo had been compelled to draw on the ever-diminishing savings he had brought from Milan. He decided grimly that since engineering did not pay it might be better to return to art.

Fortunately for the painter the Florentine government had just decided to decorate the walls of its council hall with paintings illustrating inspiring episodes in the city's history.

Leonardo received as his assignment the battle of Anghiari in 1440, a crisis for Florence, when, without loss of a single life, the city's soldiery defeated the vastly superior forces of Milan. The city fathers, after giving Leonardo the commission, reminded him of the story that Saint Peter had appeared at an opportune moment to announce that with God's aid the defenders of Florence, who had been surprised by the enemy, would be victorious.

"I can see it all," murmured a portly wool merchant, who for some reason considered himself an art critic. "Saint Peter in the center with the Florentines rallying around him and the cowardly enemy taking to flight."

Leonardo listened with polite patience to this and other instructions he had already decided to ignore. It mattered little to him whether the battle had been won by force of arms or divine intervention. His one intention was to present the horrible beauty and confusion of war as he visioned it in his "Treatise on Painting": Flying horses, maddened men . . . "and do not leave any level spot that is not trampled and soaked with blood."

As in his earlier days he drew preliminary studies of horses; but not the stately steeds that bore the Magi to the manger, nor the fiery animals which prefigured the great horse of Milan. The beasts he now sketched fled in terror or paused to fight with teeth and hoof; others writhed beside their fallen masters in the last agonies of death. The warriors were of every type: young and vigorous, old and weak. "Make the beaten and conquered pallid," Leonardo wrote for his own direction, "with brows raised and knit together . . . let the lips be arched, displaying the upper row of teeth and let the teeth be parted after the manner of such as cry in lamentation."

Although there should have been no rivalry between two men so different in their aims and achievements, Leonardo grew greatly annoyed when a commission to paint another historical mural for the council hall was assigned to another artist, Michelangelo Buonarroti.

There had been a feeling of rivalry between the two since the days when Lorenzo the Magnificent had shown no interest in Leonardo's paintings but had showered favors on the boy genius. Michelangelo had continued his career as sculptor, Leonardo as painter. Leonardo had hoped that the city fathers might find his battlepiece so acceptable that he would receive commissions for the rest of the murals intended for the council hall. When Leonardo learned that a mural had been assigned to Michelangelo, who previously had done little painting, he thought of the senseless quarrels that lay between them and felt certain that the sculptor had undertaken the work chiefly to annoy and spite him.

Leonardo had a short time before innocently offended Michelangelo, who was always ready to take offense at what he considered criticism of himself or his work. At the completion of the latter's heroic statue of the young David, there had been much controversy over a proper site for the masterpiece. Every prominent artist and sculptor in Florence had expressed his opinion, Leonardo among the rest. As always in the matter of art or science Leonardo had acted with cold impartiality. But the always-suspicious Michelangelo insisted that Leonardo da Vinci had belittled his work and wished the statue to be relegated to an obscure position.

There was no open quarrel between the two men until that late afternoon when Leonardo joined a group of his friends who sat in a public square engaged in earnest debate. The controversy raged over the interpretation of a difficult passage in one of the poems of the Florentines' best-loved poet and townsman, Dante. Turning to the newcomer, one of the debaters asked his opinion.

Leonardo shook his head. "My interpretation of the passage you have just quoted would be of little value," he answered, "since I am anything but an authority on the subject. But, look, Michelangelo is crossing the piazza. I have heard he has long been a student of Dante and is something of a poet himself. His opinion should be of real interest."

Michelangelo, who seemed about to slouch past with his usual awkward gait, suddenly turned and faced the speaker. He had evidently overheard Leonardo's remarks and assumed they were spoken in mockery. The sculptor's strong hands knotted into angry fists; his rage seemed to choke him.

Not one of the circle could fail to note the difference between the two men. Leonardo, at fifty, still carried himself with the ease of a youthful dancer; his carefully kept beard and flowing locks gleamed golden in the rays of the setting sun, his hands and linen were spotless, the dark velvet of his beret and cloak showed not a fleck of dust. His very being was imbued with a calm and dignity that seemed to prod the man before him into greater anger.

To Michelangelo nature had denied the graces she had bestowed so lavishly on the one he considered his enemy. The sculptor's face was disfigured by a broken nose, a memento of a youthful quarrel. His clothes were spotted with clay, his great hands were rough and dirty from his labors in the studio. Beneath his uncombed hair his eyes, bloodshot and restless, glared with the hatred he found so difficult to express.

At last he spat out the words that filled Leonardo da Vinci with a shame he could never quite forget: "Explain the passage yourself, you who are as learned in books as you are skilled in many arts, save the art of sculpture! For did you not labor for sixteen years with your great clay horse, hoping to cast it in bronze, but in the end abandoning it as you have so many of your works!"

He strode on, still muttering in his anger. Even if Michelangelo had lingered to continue the quarrel, it is not likely that Leonardo could have answered him. Why try to hide behind such a glib excuse as the difficulty of obtaining in war-threatened Milan enough metal to assure his statue immortality? Had he been less ambitious and contrived a smaller work, Leonardo now told himself in bitter self accusation, it might have been possible to secure the needed bronze. But as always he had sought for perfection, again and again to end his dreaming in defeat. But this time, he vowed with flashing eyes and tightened lips, this time his murals in their completeness would bring shame upon Michelangelo and his work.

After the quarrel in the city square, the sculptor had sought a commission to paint a mural in the council hall; not because he was eager to do a historical picture, suggested the gossips, but because in his conceit he felt certain that even in an unaccustomed art he would outshine his enemy. As if to lend credence to the rumor, Michelangelo chose a scene as unlike as possible the furious combat Leonardo depicted. He showed the soldiers at Anghiari, pausing in their march to bathe and rest.

If Leonardo da Vinci felt any anger at Michelangelo's choice of subject, he refused to discuss the matter. Nor did he speak freely to his associates of the joy that had come to him with his newest undertaking. For now whenever he broke off work on the battle mural, he found a strange peace in painting the picture of a lady of Florence.

Although Mona Lisa's husband, Francesco del Giocondo, was rich enough to promise handsome payment for her portrait, it was not the fee that tempted Leonardo to neglect his murals for the council hall. From the moment the young woman and the painter met he knew he could never rest until he had imprisoned on his canvas the steadfast eyes, the smile that haunted his waking hours and his dreams.

What mystery lay behind that smile? Leonardo often wondered. Or was it only the affectation of a silly, empty-headed woman of fashion? Leonardo da Vinci for all his unworldliness knew something of the foibles and frivolities of his day: the etiquette which prescribed how a gentlewoman should walk and stand and pluck her eyebrows—and never laugh outright, but only smile secretively "from the corner of her mouth."

Or could that smile be due, puzzled the anatomist, merely to the action of certain muscles that control the lips. Perhaps, he decided, if they spent long hours together while she posed for him, he might come to unravel that mystery—which might prove to be no mystery in the end.

So Leonardo consented to paint the portrait of La Gioconda. He turned gratefully from his mural, which reeked with the blood of the battlefield, to the gentle, quiet woman who in her unfailing calm seemed far remote from the battle of life. And Leonardo did all that lay in his power to deepen and intensify the peace and joy she brought to him. He arranged that certain of his pupils should lighten the weariness of her long sittings by reading aloud from the poetry of Dante or Petrarch or of some later Italian singer. Or on another day there would be music on the lyre or lute.

When the lutes grew silent, Leonardo da Vinci talked to the lady of many things: of his boyhood home in the shadow of the frowning castle at Vinci; of the bright, carefree life in Milan "before the French came down upon us"; of cities he had visited and women he had painted. He told her also quaint fables and many a droll and witty tale. To all this she listened with a child's eagerness and delight. But in return for his confidences she told him nothing of her own girlhood or the years that followed in the house of a husband who was old enough to be her father.

He touched her only when he rearranged the draperies which sometimes slipped from her shoulders or moved her wearied hands, when she left them fall from the position in which he planned to paint them. His lips never brushed that slow, mysterious smile. Yet Leonardo came nearer to loving Mona Lisa than any other woman who had ever crossed his path. But a fear, cold and inexplicable, raised a wall between them. She was too much like the mother who had been thrust into the darkness so soon that she must ever remain youthful and lovely to her yearning son. While at other times when he looked upon La Gioconda's face, Leonardo seemed to see again the tender compassion of his youthful step-mother. In spite of the longing which burned within him he was forced to banish Mona Lisa to the shadows where dwelt the two women who had ruled his boyish heart.

A day arrived when she failed to come to Leonardo's studio for her sitting. Nor did she come the next day or the day that followed. To Leonardo, who had grown perplexed and apprehensive, Salai brought back gossip he had picked up in the market place. Francesco del Giocondo, reported Salai with his knowing leer, had grown weary of Leonardo's outrageous tardiness in completing the portrait. He was reputed a jealous husband; perhaps he suspected a most unseemly reason for prolonging the sittings.

The lady never returned to Leonardo's studio. His face was bleak with loneliness while he worked with a new intensity to complete the long-delayed battle mural in the council hall of Florence. But if he grieved he shared his grief with no one. The name of La Gioconda does not appear in the secret script of Leonardo's notebooks, nor is there a single mention of her rejected portrait.

When at last Leonardo, the perfectionist, reluctantly admitted that he had finished his portrait of Mona Lisa, art lovers and even a king offered him great sums for the painting. But he refused every offer. The picture remained with him through all his wanderings to lighten the gloom of his last illness and comfort him on the day of his death.

Chapter 18

WHEN Leonardo began his anatomical studies of the muscles of the plunging horses and running men in his battle mural, as usual he allowed his enthusiasm to carry him far afield. Soon the scientist absorbed the artist. Long after the painter had completed his preliminary sketches of beasts and men, he continued to explore further and further the mysteries of the human body.

The monks of the hospital of Santa Maria Novella granted the artist-investigator permission to perform a number of anatomies. He records his revulsion at the sights and smells of the mortuary where he performed his autopsies, but he did not allow the horror he felt to deter him. To his careful investigations Leonardo added his superb artistic skill; many of the sketches he drew in these early years of the sixteenth century are greatly superior to the anatomical drawings which were to appear long after his death.

Many of Leonardo's discoveries in the fields of anatomy and physiology, and the sketches which illustrated them, would have astonished and inspired the physicians of his day had they been permitted to examine his notebooks. His studies of the heart and the bloodstream, of the human skull and of the optic nerve, establish him as a pioneer. Later physicians marveled at his description of the methods he devised of boring into the skull to study the brain without injuring the delicate tissues beneath.

The monks also permitted Leonardo to visit their patients in the hospital of Santa Maria Novella. Here he spent many hours sitting beside the beds of those who seemed most certain to die, for Leonardo believed that the study of symptoms in the living would greatly aid him in his post-mortems. Day after day he visited a very old man who seemed free from pain but continually complained of the cold. When at last the ancient died Leonardo was eager to perform an autopsy; he wondered what disease could cause so peaceful a death. The description he wrote in his notebooks after a night spent in the charnel house is another "first" in medical history; it is the first known account of a death caused by hardening of the arteries.

About the time that Leonardo made this discovery another very old man died in Florence. At his death Piero da Vinci, the notary, left ten sons and two daughters, as well as a fourth wife. He also left a considerable fortune which the grown sons tried to snatch from the minor children, the result of Piero da Vinci's last marriage. Leonardo, although he had often been assured he would share equally with the notary's legitimate sons, was not mentioned in the will.

Leonardo seldom showed the slightest interest in money affairs. Now more than ever he appeared indifferent to the loss of his hoped-for inheritance, because he was caught in the meshes of the dream which for years had haunted his waking hours—the dream of the Great Bird.

Wings shadowed him as he broke off from his memoranda on geology, on light, on architecture, and astronomy, to make notes and still more notes:

> The thrushes and other small birds are able to make headway against the course of the wind, because they fly in spurts; that is they take a long course below the wind, by dropping in a slanting direction towards the ground, with their wings half closed, and they then open the wings and catch the wind in them with their

reverse movement, and so rise to a height; and then they drop again in the same way.

Write of swimming under water and you will have the flight of the bird through the air.

Dissect the bat, study it carefully and on this model construct the machine.

You will make an anatomy of the wings of a bird together with the muscles of the breast which are the movers of these wings.

There were many sketches, also, ranging from the wings of birds with lines that indicated the resistance of their feathers against the wind to a study of the completed ornithopter with its triumphant rider.

These sketches suggested that Leonardo conceived one device after another to carry man through the air. His first design gave the operator two pairs of wings which were to be worked by the power of his arms and legs. The second completed design was clearly a helicopter, or aerial screw, which was designed to obtain lift through compressed air. And the third, which he now worked feverishly to perfect, resembled strongly framed sails on which the inventor hoped a man might actually glide for an unlimited distance.

Now in the year 1503, after many disheartening failures, Leonardo toiled with renewed excitement in his Florence workroom. There was an excellent reason for his eagerness to complete the Great Bird.

In the noisy tavern and the dim quiet of the cathedral, in the apothecary shop where Leonardo purchased a fresh supply of pigments for his battle murals, lively, though not always accurate, tongues repeated the same tale: "Yes, at Perugia. My wife's brother-in-law (or it might be my cousin's nephew, or my landlord's grandson) was in Perugia and saw what happened with his own eyes. God's mercy, what will sinners attempt next in this world which seems going straight to ruin what with plagues and war."

At this point of the narrative a listener was sure to interrupt with: "But what did happen in Perugia last January?"

"The marriage of the duke's sister—what a spectacle!—what a tourney!—with plenty of free wine and roasted meats! And to crown all, it was promised that the mathematician, Giovanni Danti, would fly from the church tower on the machine he had just invented. Fly, mind you, as though it is not enough that the good God in His wisdom has given a man two stout legs for walking. Yet he must try to fly from the tower of the church of Santa Maria della Vergine!"

"And, of course, was crushed on the stones of the pavement for his impious folly!"

"Nay, a fool's luck protected the sinner. The devil's machine actually hovered in the air for a minute and the crowd in the piazza below howled their cheers. Then it fell, fell like a broken bird. Many women fainted from horror and even strong men sickened and turned away. But it is well said that there is a special providence to care for tipplers and fools. The contrivance landed on the roof of the church. And instead of the awful death he so well deserved the inventor suffered only a broken leg. Did you ask whether he was repentant? Not he! For 'tis said that he plans, when he is fully recovered from his hurts, to attempt to fly again above the housetops."

Leonardo da Vinci listened with a passive face, but a great fear seemed to freeze his heart. What if Danti succeeded in his next attempt? It was likely that others shared the mathematician's secrets; they might rise as though borne on eagles' wings before Leonardo had completed his invention. Would the unfinished model in his workshop then become worthless? Would it become just another emblem of futility like the clay colossus, the unfinished canal to Pisa, and all the other failures that littered the highway of his disappointed years?

He shook his head stubbornly as he bent over the unfinished wings. This time he would succeed. The Great Bird would fly.

In his calculations of the weight his machine might be made to carry, and his measurements of the supporting wings, Leonardo continued to pattern his invention after the mechanism of the birds which he had observed so long and with such loving patience. Many, many years later mathematicians admiringly studied the meticulous measurements and computations they found in his notebooks. They could understand why at last even Leonardo felt satisfied.

But the ambitious Florentine's pioneer flying machine lacked the one vital element necessary for its success; it lacked the motive power to keep it aloft in the air. And the invention of small but powerful engines to generate such power was still centuries away.

It was not an atheistic inventor who gloated over the latest model in his workshop near the cathedral. Leonardo felt Messianic hopes throbbing in his breast as he penned:

> Men shall speak with and touch and embrace each other while standing each in different hemispheres, and shall understand each other's language.

Ever the mystic, his mind leaped the span of centuries. He envisioned a world where nations were no longer divided by the treacherous seas or by endless miles to be traversed by men on horseback or in lumbering coaches.

On another day, below his latest notes on improving the construction of his machine, he made a hasty sketch of the map of Europe. He sketched also on the same page the Iberian Peninsula with a list of its provinces. He felt so certain that the invention of flying would open up many possibilities for travel that he drew the first maps for the guidance of aviators.

Were these aviators to skim the skies only as ambassadors of peace and understanding between nations? Was Leonardo a seer who forced himself to face the truth no matter how bitter? For among his prophecies he wrote:

> There shall be seen huge bodies devoid of life, carrying great numbers of men with fierce speed to the destruction of their lives.

As a member of the military staff of Cesare Borgia, Leonardo had learned the horrors of war. But he seldom shrank from increasing such horrors.

He might write as poet and seer but he always remained the cool, calculating scientist. When he made the final preparations for the launching of the Great Bird on its first glad voyage through space, he considered plans for a parachute. If our friend in Perugia had had such a useful contrivance, thought Leonardo, he might have saved himself a shattered leg.

There is a mountain in Tuscany which bears the name of Monte Cecero, since its shape suggests the graceful outline of a swan. It looks down upon Fiesole, which Leonardo visited in the spring of 1506. In his notebook Leonardo da Vinci penned a secret notation in his secret script:

The Great Bird will take its first flight upon the back of the great swan, filling the whole world with amazement and filling all records with its fame; and it will bring eternal glory to the nest where it was born.

Except for another slightly altered version of this statement Leonardo never wrote a single word of his flight above Fiesole. He may have confided the story of his shattered dream to his trusted friend, Fazio Cardano; for years later when Leonardo slept in an unmarked grave in a faraway country, this scholar's son spoke of the attempted flight from the church tower at Perugia and of another, no more successful, above the mountain that resembles the swan.

"Both those who attempted to fly came to grief," records the son of Fazio Cardano. "Leonardo also tried to fly, but he too failed. He was a magnificent painter."

Although no man had seen the beginning and the end of Leonardo's flight, for many winters afterwards peasants of Fiesole as they sat about their fires repeated a tale their grandfathers had told them. It concerned the mountain whose shape resembles a swan and a Great Bird which for a moment hovered above it. The young grew wistful and envious, but their wiser elders crossed themselves in fear at the impious daring of a man who had tried to fly.

Chapter 19

IN SPITE of Leonardo da Vinci's heartbreaking disappointment on the mountain, he continued to explore and experiment.

In Milan he had experimented with various pigments that the colors of "The Last Supper" might glow in eternal brightness in spite of the dampness of the convent walls. Now, in Florence, as he at last prepared to bring his battle scene to the walls of the council chamber, he decided to ignore the well-tried methods of earlier mural painters.

A century before two Flemish brothers, Hubert and Jan Van Eyck, through much experimentation had learned that by adding oil to their pigments they could be sure of success in painting on stone and plaster. However, because Leonardo believed that the Flemish method would not produce the strong colors he desired to portray his scenes of violence, he experimented still further. He bade his assistants to varnish the walls before the paints were applied.

Although at first the colors glowed with the brilliance of jewels, Leonardo grew impatient. Why did it take so long for his greatly improved paint to dry? he asked himself. The artist decided to repeat a former experiment. He ordered an immense kettle to be filled with live coals and placed in the middle of the hall. Then he waited. As the flames rose higher and higher, the excessive heat caused the melting colors to merge in hideous pools. On the defaced surface of the ruined mural the figures of the conquerors and the conquered, stripped alike of fury and pathos, hovered like dim shadows.

For the first time in his life of splendid failures and titanic defeats Leonardo acknowledged discouragement. In deepening apathy he listened to the demands of the city fathers that he should begin work at once on the restoration of his already long-delayed commission.

"And, pray, this time be careful that your ill-timed impatience to complete your masterpiece does not ruin it!" a portly Florentine banker warned with an ill-concealed sneer.

Leonardo swung on his tormentor, who hastily covered his mouth with his gloved hand and pretended to cough. For a dangerous light glowed in the artist's eyes.

Never a patient man, Leonardo had lately grown even more short-tempered. In his disappointment and depression it seemed to the painter that his rival, Michelangelo, had returned to Florence just to plague him!

The burly, untidy giant had left his mural unfinished that he might serve Pope Julius II, but he had again quarreled with the Holy Father, whose temper matched his own, and had turned his back on Rome. Now he worked feverishly to complete his painting for the council hall.

It will be finished at the promised time, Leonardo thought bitterly. For he is a man of single purpose and allows nothing to turn him aside from a task he has once begun. Nor at the end will he destroy the work of his hands because he desires what is already good and worthy to be a little nearer perfection.

In these dark hours Leonardo found a little comfort in the youthful and generous worship of Raphael Sanzio. Among the many artists who often stood in the council hall to watch the rival painters at work, the slender, large-eyed lad from Urbino was conspicuous by his gentle, almost girlish beauty.

One day Leonardo questioned the stranger. He learned that Raphael's father, also a painter, had sent him to Florence to study under Perugino. Leonardo looked over the youth's sketches; although Raphael still dutifully copied his teacher's saints in all their prim stiffness, he had added certain poetic touches of his own.

Leonardo nodded his approval.

"I think," he said slowly, "that some day you will really be able to express yourself. Then you will be a great painter."

The boy's large, dark eyes glowed with confidence. "I hope," he answered modestly, "that my hand will always be guided as it is now by Leonardo da Vinci."

Leonardo was deeply moved. He could not know that when the years would bring this stripling fame and fortune the Urbino painter would fail to acknowledge his debt.

Soon the disappointed artist was glad to have an excuse to leave the city that had grown so hateful to him. Fortunately, even while Leonardo sought to postpone further work on the Battle of Anghiari, rescue arrived in a letter from Charles d'Amboise, the conquering French king's representative at Milan. It seemed Charles required a summer place on the outskirts of the city; he had decided it must be designed by the architect of the deposed Duke Ludovico.

There was much growling among the city rulers and hints that it was not a novelty for Leonardo da Vinci to accept a commission, pocket his fees—and seek employment elsewhere. But Charles d'Amboise was the representative of Louis XII. The king had shown himself willing to be the friend and protector of Florence; the Florentines were eager that such kindly relations should continue. Rather grudgingly the authorities granted the artist a leave of absence. But he must return in three months to repair the damages suffered by his painting. They could rely on his word, so his patrons assured Leonardo; but before he left would he please sign a promise to return, and to make everything legal, let him deposit one hundred and fifty florins. Just a formality, of course, and the money would be restored to him as soon as he returned.

Now a new and carefree life began for Leonardo in Milan, the city which in his youth he had hoped to conquer. Charles d'Amboise, although a marshal of France and grand admiral of the French navy, did not share the military leader's usual suspicion of a civilian expert. Again Leonardo talked of canals, of dredging rivers that they might become navigable, of his military inventions. Charles d'Amboise grew so enthusiastic that he insisted Leonardo's leave of absence from Florence should be extended.

"The city fathers dared to scold me like a schoolboy," Leonardo told the marshal after Charles had shown him several indignant letters from the Tuscan city. "Now they wrangle over my living remains as their forefathers quarreled for the body of Dante whom they had driven into exile."

"A word from King Louis might be helpful," suggested Charles d'Amboise.

King Louis, now the virtual ruler of Italy, obligingly wrote to the Florentine authorities that it was his royal will that Leonardo da Vinci should enter his service and remain in Milan. He was rather vague about the duties he expected Leonardo to render; the monarch had hinted he might require the painting of a madonna, or, perhaps, his own portrait. When he finally reached Milan, Louis XII was so struck by "The Last Supper" that he regretted it could not be removed from the convent and carried back to France.

"The Last Supper!" Again Leonardo had striven mightily—and had failed. The walls of the convent were damp; there was some fault in the pigments. One day shortly after his return to Milan Leonardo visited the convent. He walked the length of the refectory and stood before the painting. For a long while he gazed with the awe of a stranger upon the aloof majesty of the central figure, the clustered faces of the disciples. Then what looked like a blot in a lower corner of the mural caught his eye.

Leonardo examined what at first seemed to be a minor blemish. In growing terror he searched further, ran his hands across the painted surface. It dripped with moisture; the colors in one of the draperies had turned dim. The artist knew that the picture he had dreamed would reveal his soul through the ages had already started to fade before his disillusioned eyes.

While in Milan, Leonardo was saddened by the news of the death of his Uncle Francesco. The kind old man had always loved the disinherited and sometimes wayward son of the da Vinci household. Now he left Leonardo the greater part of his property. This meant much to the disinherited son of Piero da Vinci. My uncle truly loved me, he thought. And, exulted Leonardo, by his legacy he acknowledges me as a member of the family!

Although he had not visited his uncle for many years, Francesco's death saddened Leonardo who, with his passing, felt the last link with his kindred was broken. The friends of his youth had died or were widely scattered; his protégé, Salai, showed no gratitude for many benefits and kept in touch with Leonardo only to receive more gifts.

But in these last years in Milan two friendships blessed and comforted the lonely man.

These two friends were younger than Leonardo. Francesco Melzi was hardly more than a boy. He had sought Leonardo da Vinci for instruction in painting. Possessed of little talent, he might have left the studio shortly but remained to serve the aging master with the zeal of a disciple and the devotion of a son.

Francesco asked for nothing, for his father's recent death had left him with ample means. The studio-workshop, now that Leonardo was growing old, was no longer gay with music and boyish voices. But Francesco neither desired nor sought companions of his own age. It was enough for him that he might serve the man he loved as secretary, oversee the affairs of the household, and, on the rare occasions when Leonardo seemed in the mood, to sit at his feet in the twilight and listen to his tales of other days. It was a quiet existence for a young man of good blood with many careers to choose from. But Francesco Melzi loved Leonardo and was content.

The second friend, younger than Leonardo but considerably older than Francesco, was in spite of his youth one of the leading anatomists and scholars of his day. Marcantonio della Torre, as a professor at the universities of Pisa and Padua, had attracted not only the most advanced students but also many of the unlearned. They were drawn at first by curiosity to hear him lecture and returned again and again to enjoy his clear and startlingly original expositions and to watch his demonstrations.

Like Leonardo, Marcantonio was so deeply immersed in his own research that he paid no heed to the wars and rebellions that seethed about him. In spite of his lack of interest in political affairs, certain spy hunters at Padua accused him of conspiring against the state of Venice, which controlled the university. So in 1510 Leonardo found him teaching in Pavia, so close to Milan that he was able to attend della Torre's lectures.

"In this winter," Leonardo jotted down confidently, "I hope to master the whole field of anatomy." With the knowledge and inspiration he gained from Marcantonio, a scholar as exacting and even more consecrated than himself, Leonardo da Vinci felt it would be possible to prepare for publication his own extensive studies in anatomy along with their really revolutionary illustrations.

But as so often before he was forced to face the bitter truth of an old poet's lament: "The life so short, the art so long to learn." In those overburdened years in Milan he turned from the designing of the grand marshal's summer palace to many things. He painted Leda with her downcast eyes and enigmatic smile. He planned locks for the canal of Saint Christopher. He had long been interested in the draining of marshes. Why should men die like flies of swamp fever? he asked indignantly and for a little while devoted himself to the problem. In one of his studies on hydraulics he described the conditions that produced swamps and suggested how the air above might be cleansed and the marshes themselves transformed into productive land. Then a new project caught his fancy; soon another. In this, his second Milanese period, the engineer and inventor jotted down so many ideas it would have taken several methodical geniuses a lifetime to develop all of them completely.

But when was Leonardo da Vinci ever methodical? He seemed to forget land reclamation while he discussed the intricacies of miniature painting with a court painter of King Louis. He seriously considered printing a number of his notebooks; for the purpose he actually invented a printing press, which was greatly superior to those then in use. But he seemed to shrink from the mammoth task of sorting and revision and continued to add still more closely covered sheets to the pile between the bulging covers.

King Louis XII regularly paid his royal engineer a pension which made Leonardo willing to forfeit the sum he had left behind to insure his return to Florence. The monarch had many benevolent plans for restoring the prosperity of the states his armies had ravaged; he approved heartily of many of Leonardo da Vinci's proposals. But the days of France's sovereignty in the conquered territory were rapidly drawing to a close.

For years the invading French armies had swept over Italy. Often they met no resistance from the tiny, disunited city-states. Sometimes the populace, long sullen under foreign tyranny, would rise against the invaders. But before long another army, made strong by reinforcements, would again batter down the city's gates.

There was one Italian patriot who never lost hope in ultimate victory. Pope Julius II had the heart of a warrior. When Michelangelo painted his portrait, the fearless pontiff commanded him: "Put in my hand not a book but a sword!" His enthusiasm drew many to fight under his banner. "I will wager a hundred ducats and my tiara on top of them," he pledged, "that I shall drive the French out of Italy."

Charles d'Amboise, in whose headquarters at Milan Leonardo had lived as an honored guest, died suddenly. His successor, Marshal Trivulzio, who had in his turn befriended the artist, in 1512 joined the retreating French. Under the protection of the victorious German Emperor Maximilian, his young godson, Maximiliano Sforza returned to claim the family throne. Duke Ludovico's eldest son was a handsome stripling with much of his father's charm, decided Leonardo, as he noted how well the boy sat his horse and how graciously he received the plaudits of the happy Milanese.

But the young duke, although loved by his people, ruled for only a little while in Lombardy. News came that the French troops had again crossed the frontier and like his unhappy father so many years before he fled from Milan to escape his enemies. More fortunate than Duke Ludovico, young Maximiliano found safety in Switzerland.

This time the French invaders were driven back. By the autumn of 1513 their last garrison in Milan, sick and discouraged and starving, surrendered.

Sometime before Louis XII had cut off Leonardo's pension. He could hope for little from the new government, weak and uncertain and impoverished from war. Who in Milan would employ him either as engineer or painter? Even if he could have earned a comfortable living in the Lombard capital, Leonardo felt he could never again be truly happy in the city that had been his home for so many years. He knew Milan would never seem the same without the two dear friends he had lost there, the bluff soldier, Charles d'Amboise and Marcantonio della Torre. The saintly scholar had died as nobly as he had lived; during a plague, which swept the city, he had sacrificed his own life in caring for the stricken.

For a little while Leonardo dreamed of returning to Florence. But he felt certain that in the city of his youth he would face open hostility. After the long-drawn-out quarrel with the authorities over the unfinished murals, it seemed wiser to seek employment elsewhere.

There was only one city in Italy, he decided, where he might hope to continue his work. The fiery warrior, Pope Julius II, was dead; his successor, Pope Leo X, a member of the Medici family, like all his brethren loved and patronized the arts. Pope Leo had sent for Michelangelo of Florence, Raphael Sanzio of Urbino and many other artists and architects to carry on the rebuilding and beautification of Rome begun by Pope Julius.

Leonardo bade several of his favorite pupils help him gather together his unfinished canvases and uncompleted notebooks. In one of the half-filled volumes he recorded:

I left Milan for Rome on the 24th day of September, 1513.

It was the last of many mistakes in a life which had been marked by many errors.

Autumn

in Rome

"Alas! who do I see? The Savior crucified again."
                    —*from the notebooks of Leonardo da Vinci*

Chapter 20

$\mathcal{T}$O LEONARDO DA VINCI'S quickly disillusioned eyes Rome appeared a city aglow with nightmarish beauty.

At first his senses were so ravished with the loveliness of the Belvedere Gardens that stretched below the windows of his studio that Leonardo was strangely blind to the decay and corruption time and evil men had brought to the Eternal City. Pope Leo X had sent for rare plants from many countries; the gardeners of the Vatican had tended the alien flowers and shrubs so zealously that the gardens of the summer palace in the city of the Popes soon became one of its showplaces. Leonardo discovered this new treasure house of exotic plants, shrubs, and trees shortly after his arrival. For several days he could do little but walk up and down the winding paths, admiring a flower or bush he could not classify.

Later the urge of the botanist, latent so many years, grew so strong that he began to sketch and describe what he saw. It was not until he had filled several pages of a new notebook with floral drawings that Leonardo turned his attention to the many statues that gleamed white against the trees and hedges. Leonardo pointed out to Melzi the huge allegorical group that portrayed Father Tiber;

139

he told the youth that the Venus was one of the earliest pagan statues rescued from the ruins to grace a modern garden.

A few days later master and pupil visited another collection of rarities that added not a little to the fame and glory of Leo X, ruler over the Christian world. In the pope's menagerie were gathered more unfamiliar animals than Leonardo had ever seen in a single zoo. There were panthers and leopards and, of course, many lions; various rulers had not been above punning on the name the pope had assumed on his coronation. Leonardo was eager to study the apes and certain forlorn little monkeys that huddled, frightened and homesick, in the next cage.

"And, master, see the white elephant which the king of Portugal sent the Holy Father!" cried Francesco Melzi. "While you were watching the caged birds, the keeper told me that the beast understands every word that is spoken in his presence."

"How long did it take him to learn Italian?" asked Leonardo very gravely.

"I do not know," answered Melzi, glad to hear his friend jesting again, for Leonardo had been so withdrawn since their arrival in Rome. "But I warn you to take no risks and to mind your tongue before his elephantine majesty. For the keeper, who makes him his special care, told me also that the beast is the Pope's favorite and it would go ill with anyone who annoyed or teased him. Perhaps you will not believe this either, but the keeper told me also that when Pope Leo first came out to see the elephant, the creature knelt politely at his feet, raised his trunk, and saluted his Holiness three times—then dipped into a tub of water and soaked him from head to foot. But the Pope had already grown so fond of his new pet that he forgave him."

"As one good Christian should forgive another," commented Leonardo. "Do not worry, Francesco, you surely noticed how I lowered my voice. So it is not likely our mischievous friend overheard me and will carry tales to the Holy Father. Ah, these gardens are truly a wonderland and I wonder which will afford me the greater pleasure to study and explore—the strange flowers or these stranger beasts. And how beautifully the evening shadows fall on those wide plains, which turn to purple at our feet."

Leonardo da Vinci dropped his hand on the young man's shoulder; his voice trembled slightly with emotion. "A place to study! A place of beauty and of peace! God grant I may spend the last years of my life here, Francesco."

And Francesco Melzi silently echoed the master's prayer.

But as the days passed and Leonardo left his retreat at the Belvedere to wander about the great city he saw and heard many things to disquiet him.

It hurt him to see pigs rooting in the filth and ruins of the once magnificent Forum, or cattle pastured in the shadow of the tomb of the Emperor Augustus. Shortly after their arrival in Rome Melzi had returned from the market to tell Leonardo indignantly: "When I bought this fish I noticed the fishmonger had strewn his wares on a beautiful marble table. I wondered to see it put to such a base purpose and asked him how he had come by it. The fellow laughed and said: 'One of my neighbors did dig a privy and he unearthed some urns and this table which a passing scholar declared was used as an altar in a pagan temple. So I bought it cheaply for displaying my fish and it has served me well."

"Does that shock you?" asked Leonardo with a grim smile. "An oaf spreads his stinking fish on an altar from a long buried temple —and rejoices at the bargain he has made. He knows no better. But what of my fellow Florentine, Bramante, who less than a dozen years ago was chosen as architect for the new church of Saint Peter? An artist should serve beauty, not destroy it. I know that some of the ancient buildings were tottering; they were dead shells that had become a menace to the living. But Bramante was needlessly ruthless in his destruction. It hurts me, my son, to see the stones of what were once noble temples and theaters and the mausoleums of the mighty dead built into the foundations of dwellings for pygmies of our own day."

To Leonardo da Vinci even a greater insult to the long-departed glory which had once been Rome were the miserable, tumbling hovels of the poor; they seemed to spring like hideous mushrooms among the ruins. Never before had he seen such degrading poverty. As he walked through the slums that bordered the Tiber, Leonardo tried not to see the dirty, diseased children who played in the gutter, and their mothers, slovenly and prematurely aged. Swamp fever—so the physicians called the malaria that crept up from the Pontine Marshes—added its cruelty to the heartlessness of man.

If one could drain those marshes, which menaced not only the forgotten poor but the princes and the cardinals in their gracious gardens beyond the Tiber! But who would listen to an obscure and discredited engineer?

He tried to forget such horrors by visiting the gorgeous Vatican library, the Sistine Chapel. Here Michelangelo had daily stretched himself on his high platform for four agonizing years to paint the ceiling for the greater glory of Pope Julius. Now Leonardo gazed upon his rival's work and tried to crush the envy which welled up in his discouraged heart.

Francesco Melzi, who stood beside Leonardo, looked with wonder at his master's pale face, usually so calm but now quivering with emotion. At last he dared to speak. He tried to choose his words carefully, for in the gossip of the studios he had learned something of the hatred that existed between the two men.

"I have heard this called one of the greatest paintings in the world," said Franceso Melzi. "But," loyally, "I am not sure until I hear your verdict."

"You should learn to judge for yourself," Leonardo answered with unwonted sternness. "I hope I shall never be like so many of the empty-pated fools who pilgrimage here and think that all they find in Rome merits the wildest praise. After I have come many times to study these figures, ask me again and I shall try to answer you honestly. But now—now I can say only that they are worthy of Michelangelo."

He threw back his head that he might study the pictures on the ceiling. Suddenly the look of intense concentration disappeared and lines of laughter crinkled the skin below Leonardo's eyes.

"Our genius has the manners of a bear," Leonardo told Francesco. "And even in his more playful moments he indulges in the tricks of that clumsy animal. Have you observed the face of God the Father seated above the throng in all His majesty? You have? Then look again and carefully at poor old Noah, drunk on his own grapes. Do you see . . ."

"Michelangelo used the same model for both," cried the horrified Melzi.

"Yes, both the Highest One and the meanest of the sinners have the face of Pope Julius II. Michelangelo quarreled with him, you know, and this seems to be his revenge."

"But did the Holy Father ever suspect . . . ?" Melzi was too shocked to continue.

"It is likely," Leonardo answered, "that more than one toady of the papal court hurried to report to Julius that the Almighty bore his features. A pretty compliment! But who would dare hint that there was the slightest resemblance between the sottish Noah and His Holiness?"

"But surely Pope Julius must have noticed . . ."

Leonardo grimaced. "Then he kept silent, which shows that he was a far better diplomat than Michelangelo!"

The next day Leonardo da Vinci was informed that Pope Leo would grant him audience.

He smiled a little at the Swiss guards who at first barred his entrance into the Pope's reception room and asked his business there. These mercenaries who for a price protected and served his Holiness were red-faced and broad-shouldered, better fitted by nature, Leonardo thought, to drive a plow or dig in a quarry than to parade in uniforms of white and green and gold. Rather gaudy, he considered them. Could the guards' dress have been designed by Michelangelo, who was sometimes overfond of flashy colors? These uniforms, so unsuited to the bulky bodies and the heavy faces of the Pope's protectors, reminded the artist of the frivolous suits he himself had contrived for one of Il Moro's tourneys or for a masquerade of Duchess Beatrice.

Leonardo da Vinci sighed a little as he passed into the reception

room. The merry, dancing duchess had followed the bright brocades and glittering ornaments she so loved into the dust. This was
no time to think of the end of all her foolish husband's pageantry!
But vandals had sacked Rome itself more than once and the artist's
eye, which is also the seer's, visioned a ravished city that even an
army of devoted Swiss mercenaries could not save.

The sumptuously decorated reception hall which led directly
into the Pope's private apartments buzzed with the comments, some
good-natured, some peevish, of the many suitors gathered there for
audience with his Holiness. These suitors were a motley crew
ranging from bored courtiers and haughty ambassadors, confident
of being the first to be granted a hearing, to humbler folk like
Leonardo da Vinci, an artist with sketches to submit to the pontiff,
or a poet who had just written an ode in honor of the accession of
Pope Leo X.

Among these suitors strayed a shabby but impudent-mannered
old man who had managed to talk his way past the Swiss guards
at the entrance. On a tray he carried a collection of crucifixes so
crudely carved that Leonardo, shuddering, turned his eyes away.
But he smiled grimly as the hawker approached one foreign visitor
after another with the suggestion: "Buy a crucifix which the Holy
Father will bless. It will protect you on your journey homeward
and be a most precious gift for those who wait your return. Buy
a crucifix carved for you by a Roman master."

He should be doused in the Tiber for daring to sell such ugliness, thought Leonardo. Yet he offers appropriate wares. For in
no other city have I seen our Savior sold so often and at so low
a price.

Leonardo was roused from his musing by a tug at his sleeve
and a plaintive voice at his ear. He turned to look at the client
who sat beside him on the long marble bench, a meek little man
in shabby but clean and well-patched garments. On his knees he
held a portfolio bulging with papers.

"I have waited here since early morning," he complained. "If
only his Holiness will be pleased to look over my plans for a new
concert hall," and his nervous fingers lovingly smoothed a sheet

couraged artist. Yesterday Raphael would have been glad to clean my brushes after I finished a day's work on my battle murals; today he paints the Pope and his cardinals and has succeeded Bramante as the architect of Saint Peter's. But tomorrow . . . if I succeed with the picture Pope Leo has commissioned me to paint . . . !

Leonardo had brooded long and bitterly over his failure with varnishes in Florence. One morning while he strolled through the gardens of the Belvedere to gather unusual plants for his botanical studies, he was seized with a new idea. He would experiment on a varnish mixed with plant juices; he would use it for the picture that the Pope had just ordered. If this time he succeeded, he would be rewarded not only by colors of enamel-like brilliancy but would know the joy of discovering a formula for really durable pigments.

As always, Leonardo tried to work in secrecy. But what secret was safe in Rome, the city of peering eyes and wagging tongues? Word came to Pope Leo that Leonardo da Vinci, even before he started work on the commissioned picture, had, as usual, put the cart before the horse and experimented with some foolish varnish. Leo's gossips from Florence and Milan knew plenty of stories of Leonardo's dilatory habits.

"He will never get anything done," Leo X pronounced judgment, "for he is always thinking about the end before he begins."

Echoes of the Pope's amusement and the resultant jibes of his court reached Leonardo in the apartment where he had hoped to be so happily employed. Although neither a courtier nor a diplomat, Leonardo da Vinci realized how ridicule can often prove fatal to a promising career. He took no further interest in the picture Pope Leo had ordered, for he felt certain that it would not win the approval of his Holiness.

Why try to compete with Raphael Sanzio? Leonardo asked himself wearily. But how employ the still restless brain and hands?

Fortunately Giuliano de' Medici remembered his promise to support Leonardo in Rome until the day he made his own fortune. He continued to pay Leonardo a monthly sum sufficient to keep up his household and hired a German workman to assist him.

that protruded from his portfolio. "Small, for just a few intimates. A little gem. You see," he confided, "a humble architect like me would never win the notice of Pope Leo with an ambitious project like, say, a refectory or another bath. Have you heard of the murals Raphael of Urbino has painted for the bath of Cardinal . . . Oh, you are a newcomer to Rome? What was I saying?" he rattled on. "Oh yes, my design for a little concert hall. Even a foreigner like you knows that the Holy Father is passionately interested in music."

"Pope Leo is a true son of Lorenzo the Magnificent," said Leonardo. "I remember how years ago the Medicis . . ."

"Not only music!" piped up another suitor, who sat just beyond the hopeful architect. Leonardo noticed that he also was lean and shabby and carried a sheaf of papers. "His Holiness dearly loves hunting. Now, if I could only attract his attention as a friend of mine did several months ago. He wrote a little pamphlet on the worming of dogs; a groom, who cares for the Pope's hunting hounds, discussed the new method with his Holiness. And now my friend has an excellent post *with a regular salary* in the papal stables. But I, alas, write only poetry."

"And I am only an artist," confessed Leonardo da Vinci with mock humility.

For once the languid and effeminate Giuliano spoke wi[...]
sion. He was a lover of Florence and proud of her many [...]
sons. As soon as he received the appointment from the [...]
Chief Captain and Standard Bearer of the Church of [...]
Giuliano renewed his promise to work for Leonardo's advan[...]

A word from this influential friend had secured the atte[...]
one even more influential in papal circles, Cardinal Bibbie[...]
had grown up in the household of Lorenzo the Magnifice[...]
had carried into his later life the friendship of the Medic[...]
Now Bibbiena was Pope Leo's most trusted political advise[...]

Young Raphael was a favorite of the Pope, who often [...]
other artists. But Leo seemed at first inclined to play the [...]
patron to the newcomer from Milan. Anxious to please his [...]
he at once commissioned Leonardo to paint a picture f[...]

He would not be easy to work with, the artist decided [...]
first interview. The pontiff, obese and aloof, seemed to lack [...]
and friendliness. He dropped several criticisms of Miche[...]
which Leonardo, in spite of his own opinion of his rival [...]
be unjust. And he overpraised young Raphael! Now L[...]
grew unjust in turn. He remembered the boy from U[...]
stripling with a madonna's face, awkward and ill at ease[...]
studios of Florence. Now by the grace of God—and Br[...]
Raphael's countryman—the upstart, as Leonardo considere[...]
ael, was the leading artist in all Rome.

Smiled upon by Pope Leo and Cardinal Bibbiena, Rapl[...]
besieged by every aristocratic visitor to Rome to do his [...]
They paid well for the distinction of sitting for the papal [...]
It was rumored that the artist who had just passed his [...]
birthday received the princely sum of twelve thousand du[...]
every room he decorated in the Vatican. He lived like a [...]
surrounded by a little court of toadies and flatterers.

The youth from Urbino had once publicly admired L[...]
now he offered to secure him commissions he was far t[...]
to execute himself. But his manner had grown so conde[...]
that Leonardo considered his friendliness an insult.

The wheel of fortune has not ceased spinning, thought[...]

Chapter 21

*F*OR three days Leonardo da Vinci waited more or less patiently for an audience with Pope Leo. When at last his name was
called and he rose stiff from cramp to enter the inner chambers,
he cast a pitying look on the two companions who had shared his
boredom. The architect and the poet still crouched in their accustomed places in all their shabby misery. Some months later Leonardo met the poet begging in the street and took him home to
dinner. He never learned what became of the architect with his
plans for a little concert hall.

But these unfortunates were not armed with the instrument
which had accomplished Leonardo's entrance—letters of recommendation from Giuliano de' Medici of Florence, the Pope's favorite brother. Giuliano had shown himself a true friend.

"It is not too late for you to make your fortune," he had advised
Leonardo. "The new city of the popes has long been abuilding but
it will rise to greater splendor since men like Bramante and Michelangelo have brought the glories of the Renaissance from Florence
to Rome. And you, a true Florentine, in spite of all your wanderings, must add to that glory."

Just as during his last years in Milan he had been seized by the urge to gain further knowledge in anatomy, now Leonardo felt a renewal of his old urge for invention. He triumphantly produced a machine for cutting screws; he designed a die for cutting the coins issued by the Vatican, and boasted that his invention not only saved labor but produced more perfectly rounded coins. He spent hours in experimenting with quicksilver, copper, and iron.

Sometimes in his soul weariness and frustration Leonardo turned from his serious labors to manufacture the "playthings" he had once so despised. But now instead of a feathered cloak for a lovely lady or a theatrical heaven, bright with stars, he fashioned monsters as unusual and terrible as the painted creature of his boyhood.

When one of the Belvedere gardeners discovered an unusually large lizard sunning itself near a fountain, Leonardo covered it with fish scales, attached horns to its head and for good measure added a tiny beard and quivering quicksilver wings. He tamed it easily, for he had a strange power over birds and beasts and creeping creatures. When visitors came to the studio, Leonardo took a childish pleasure in watching their terror of his friendly monster.

He performed grotesque tricks with sheep entrails which he inflated and caused to move as though by their own power. At another time Leonardo molded tiny figures of wax, gave them wings filled with heated air, and sent them soaring through space as though in mockery of the Great Bird with drooping pinions.

When Francesco Melzi warned his master that there were rumors that he dabbled in black magic, Leonardo laughed heartily. But when he answered Francesco he lowered his voice, for he had quickly learned not to trust his German apprentice who slept in the next room.

"Black magic! So now they accuse me of witchcraft? Because I spent hours watching the antics of the white elephant; perhaps, now that he has eaten himself into a glutton's grave, I shall be accused of casting spells to bring about his death."

"Master, this is no joking matter."

"I agree with you. For as usual the star-blessed Raphael has profited by another's misfortunes—this time the elephant's. Only this morning I heard that the beast's death has brought the Holy Father's favorite a new commission. Pope Leo has decided that his precious elephant must be immortalized and has ordered Raphael to paint the brute, larger than life, on the wall of one of the Vatican apartments."

Melzi refused to be diverted. "But, master, when it causes malicious gossip, why must you . . . ?"

"To amuse myself!" Leonardo spoke sharply. "When his Holiness, like any earthly king, has his hunchbacks and dwarfs, why should I not take my pleasure with the ugly and the misshapen? And the creatures I create to amuse myself are not aware of their ugliness. I do not employ them as court fools and shame them with my mockery."

Francesco Melzi never knew whether the master, in spite of his seeming defiance, decided as a matter of prudence to bring his manufacture of monsters to an abrupt end. Whatever the reason, Leonardo suddenly seemed to tire of the sport and put aside his play with sheep entrails and waxen figures. He stripped the lizard of all its weird trappings and carried it back to the fountain in the Belvedere Gardens.

"He should have strange tales to tell his fellow lizards of the animal we call 'man,'" Leonardo told the younger man with a smile that had lately grown bleak and bitter.

Suddenly Leonardo seemed to rouse himself sufficiently to make one more effort to win Pope Leo's approval. The pope was no judge of painting, Leonardo said to himself, and moreover was prejudiced because of the unfortunate matter with the varnish. But Leo was an acknowledged musician and deeply interested in musical science. Surely, he would welcome Leonardo's provocative "Treatise on Speech," which was based on exhaustive research on the trachea, larynx, and mouth. This essay Leonardo hopefully delivered to the Pope's privy chamberlain.

"If you could persuade his Holiness just to glance over the beginning," the scientist suggested eagerly. "I am sure that with his interest in singing he will read to the end and send for me to discuss the matter further."

The chamberlain, constantly beset by suitors to the pope, promised politely that he would do his best. Leonardo never knew whether Pope Leo ever received the essay with its painstakingly drawn illustrations. When at last he approached the chamberlain, the functionary gave him short and evasive answers.

It was about this time that Isabella d'Este made her first triumphal visit to Rome. She was entertained by the highest and mightiest; she was honored by an invitation to join the pope's own select hunting party; safely anonymous in her black mask, she romped through the pre-Lenten carnival like a peasant girl.

The great lady not only played, she attended services at every church in or near the Eternal City; she found time, with all her frivolities, to engage in what had always been her greatest pleasure —entertaining poets and musicians and artists. When she again met Leonardo da Vinci she treated him coolly, for she was not a woman to forget a slight. He did not hold his head so high as in the days back at Mantua, she observed. Now she would not have to plead with him to paint her portrait! She decided it would be wiser to employ the fashionable idol of all Rome, Raphael Sanzio.

But there was one who clasped Leonardo's hand in friendship and seemed glad to talk of other days. Atalante Miglioretti had come to Rome in the train of Isabella of Mantua, for the cultured lady refused to travel without her court poet and her favorite lute-player. The handsome youth who had been Leonardo's dear companion in Florence had but lately recovered from an attack of the treacherous marsh fever. His friend was so shocked at his altered appearance that he thoughtlessly exclaimed: "Alas, but even you have grown old!"

Atalante Miglioretti smiled sadly: "There is only a year's difference in our ages, my dear Leonardo. I am the younger and I have just reached sixty."

That night, alone in his bedchamber, Leonardo da Vinci, with a lighted taper in his hand, stood for a long time before one of his mirrors. Since his sixtieth birthday he had sometimes wondered at his unaccountable spells of weariness, a painful stiffness of his right hand. But until his reunion with Miglioretti he had not thought of himself as old. Now he forced himself to consider with another's eyes his graying hair, his many wrinkles. Like his friend he too smiled sadly at the changes time had wrought.

After Atalante Miglioretti departed for Mantua, Leonardo suffered from a strange depression. More than ever he missed his friend and patron, Giuliano de' Medici, who had departed for Savoy to marry a French princess. The elegant, pleasure-loving young magnifico and the aging painter shared much in common— a deep strain of mysticism, a passionate love of the arts. Francesco Melzi with all his devotion could not take the place of lute-player or of prince.

The German assistant, now that Leonardo's patron was absent, began to make unreasonable demands. In spite of an earlier contract, he claimed a higher salary. When this was refused, the insolent fellow managed to find many ways to annoy and bully his master. He neglected his work; refused to eat at Leonardo's table where he might have learned Italian and taught his employer German. And, crime of crimes in the eyes of Leonardo who abhorred hunting, he roamed among the ruins to shoot birds.

Leonardo tried to forget his annoyance by experimenting in his laboratory. He revised his earlier studies on the laws of gravitation; he prepared to complete his study on the flight of birds. In this connection he made a careful investigation of air currents; he performed various experiments in the field of hydraulics. He longed to continue his studies in anatomy, but now a new obstacle confronted him.

Some enemy—Leonardo believed it was his own workman— complained to the pope that Leonardo da Vinci had transgressed church law by his impious dissection of human bodies. Even in Rome this pronouncement of an earlier pope had been long ignored. Leonardo might have continued his human dissections uninterrupted had Leo X not heard rather certain disquieting stories. Certainly the scientist was not a dabbler in witchcraft, decided Pope Leo, but undoubtedly a scoffer who, unless he behaved more discreetly, might find himself investigated by the Inquisition. Meanwhile, decreed the pontiff, no more autopsies.

Leonardo wrote to his protector, Giuliano de' Medici, who had recently returned to Florence with his bride. But the generous-hearted prince was no longer able to assist his friends. Never robust, his long journey had weakened him and Giuliano lay on his death-bed.

Leonardo knew that he should no longer remain in Rome. Even with the patronage of the pope's brother, there had been little advancement. But where could he go? Should he return in humiliation to his botched battle murals in Florence? In Milan, which he had once entered proud and confident—who would offer encouragement and employment? Not so many years ago, he thought, King Louis granted me a pension that I might live in Milan and serve him and his friends. But King Louis is dead and there is no one I can appeal to.

He opened the newest of his notebooks. Lately he had made many sketches on a subject that had long fascinated him through its terror and mystery—the Deluge. His tired eyes scanned picture after picture of roaring torrent and mounting wave.

Time like a great river has swept all my hopes away, Leonardo da Vinci murmured. He thought of his high hopes when Lorenzo the Magnificent had praised his lute and promised to speak in his behalf to the ruler of Milan. Yes, years ago a Medici had smiled on him. . . .

And now the son of Lorenzo the Magnificent, a younger Medici who wore the papal crown, had turned against the man whom his father had once befriended. Leonardo drew an unfinished page toward him and penned another entry: "The Medici created and destroyed me." He felt that he had written his own epitaph.

But the next day he was ready to begin a new life in a new land. For Francis I, the successor to King Louis XII, sent Leonardo an urgent invitation to come to France.

Winter

in Amboise

"While I thought I was learning to live, I
have been learning to die"
    —*from the notebooks of Leonardo da Vinci*

Chapter 22

LEONARDO DA VINCI had reached his sixty-fourth year when he set out for the last of his many journeys. Francesco Melzi, as ever careful of all things that concerned the master, had securely tied the huge notebooks together and wrapped several of Leonardo's paintings. Leonardo's two old servants, Battista and Mathurine, who had agreed to accompany him to France, bustled importantly from wardrobe to chest as they collected clothes and paintbrushes, writing materials, and the tools the scientist had invented through the years.

"And all my cooking pots," insisted Mathurine. "Well," she compromised when Melzi insisted that the baggage would prove far too heavy, "at least my favorite stewing kettle. I have used it so long that I would never be able to prepare the master's sauce in another pot. No, do not set it aside with the brazier. I'll not let it out of my sight. If it were lost or stolen I'd never be able to get another like it in all France."

Battista patted her shoulder with a patronizing air. "Don't you know that King Francis could afford to give you a set of stewing kettles made of pure gold?" he asked.

157

What manner of man was King Francis I, at whose bidding Leonardo now traveled the icy windswept roads into France?

In his early twenties Francis was the very embodiment of the warmth, the color, and the eager enthusiasms of the Renaissance. Fatherless in childhood, he had been trained for kingship by his mother, Louise of Savoy, whose hopes for her son darkened at the successive births of the children of King Charles. But death had been Louise's ally and when Louis XII died, the ambitious, impatient woman rejoiced to see her boy mount the vacant throne.

To Francis, after a boyhood darkened with uncertainties, his kingship opened a world that was as gay and colorful as the designs of knightly tournaments his mother had embroidered in her bored widowhood in the castle of Amboise. Flushed with triumph, lusty with youth, he greeted a life of mimic or actual warfare, both equally exciting. His days were crowded with hunting, his nights with dancing and feasting and court masques.

Francis rode and fenced superbly; even if he had not been king, the courtiers would have praised his skill in hunting and on the tourney field. He was tall, handsome, and had cultivated a honeyed tongue. Not only his mother and his learned and beautiful sister, Marguerite de Valois, regarded him with a near idolatry; he was worshiped by every woman he encountered, old and young, court lady or scullery maid.

In spite of the young king's preoccupation with hunting and dancing, he found time to read widely if not intensively; he had dabbled in languages and could discuss art and philosophy fluently, if not with authority, with Leonardo da Vinci. He loved poetry and himself wrote passable verses to his fair partners of the court balls.

Never wholly mature, Francis I would become as happily excited as any child over the most absurd playthings. Some of Leonardo da Vinci's rivals for the king's favor insisted that Francis had appointed the Florentine as court painter not because of his reputation as an artist but rather as the inventor of amusing toys. In explanation these rivals described the young king's delight when at the castle of Argenton a huge lion appeared before him to the pretty terror of all the ladies. Propelled by clockwork, the beast stalked down the great hall, stopped before the king's chair, and from his breast showered a deluge of lilies.

It is like the old days when I planned spectacles for Il Moro in Milan, Leonardo thought sadly. Must I spend the few precious hours that are left to me on playthings? He forced himself to bow graciously and to smile his thanks when King Francis, the lovely hostess, Marguerite de Valois, and the entire court burst into wild applause.

The old artist was not too unhappy in what some have called his exile. But how can one be called an exile from home when all his life he has never really known a homeland? From his earliest years Leonardo, rebel and seeker, had, through the power of his genius, ranged not only over every land but the still unexplored universe. Italy or any other country would have been far too narrow an abiding place for such a restless spirit.

Yet even Leonardo, far from all accustomed scenes and his few remaining friends, might have felt lonely in France if from the first he had not encountered so much to remind him of Italy.

Francis, like all high-born Frenchmen and Englishmen of his day, was a passionate admirer of all things Italian. One story tells that the young king while in Venice begged Federico, son of Isabella d'Este, to write to his mother to send him a doll clad exactly as the ladies were at Mantua, "so that the French ladies might be able to copy them." From the country which was the first to blossom under the rich influences of the Renaissance Francis imported artists and musicians, architects and even gardeners. When Leonardo first saw the mulberry trees that grew about Amboise he turned smilingly to Francesco.

"I have learned that this garden was planned by a countryman of ours from Naples," he said. "Poor Duke Ludovico! Though some called him 'the Moor' because of his complexion, others insisted the name honored the mulberry trees which brought such wealth to Milan. Have you noticed how friendly the gardeners are? Nearly all of them are Italians and are eager to talk of the country they still consider their home."

King Francis not only granted Leonardo an annual sum generous enough to care for all his wants but authorized that his companion, Francesco Melzi, should receive a pension. Shortly after Leonardo's arrival in France, the king visited Amboise, one of his favorite palaces since he had spent much of his childhood there. Chattering like a schoolboy, Francis led his aged friend from room to room.

"Here my tutor, poor soul, tried to keep me at my books; but it was an easy matter, when his back was turned, to climb from that window ledge to the branch of yonder oak. Then I'd slip to the ground and off I'd go to the stables to visit the hounds and horses.

"And in this hall near the fireplace I spent many a rainy afternoon playing chess with my sister. Some say she is the most beautiful woman in all France. Ah, but you should have seen her then with her blue eyes flashing with excitement and her long golden hair falling over the chessboard! My lady mother worked on her tapestry as she sat in that chimney nook. I still remember how she used to sigh when she looked at us. How she feared for our futures— that I would never be king . . . and Marguerite . . . How could our mother know that my sister would be so unhappy in her marriage?

"And now," King Francis rambled on, "now I myself will conduct you to your new home. The chateau of Cloux is just a short distance down the road. A pleasant walk, but if you have grown weary . . ."

Leonardo da Vinci shook his gray head. His legs ached sorely after the tour of the palace, but he was ashamed to complain before the king's youthful buoyancy.

"I want to see the river in this early twilight," he answered. "The air here is not so clear as I remember it in Florence but the Loire is much like the Arno after sunset."

Leonardo, for all his growing weariness, refused to rest until, under the king's guidance, he had inspected the chateau at Cloux. It was a sturdy brick structure with a pointed roof and a tower and had been built by an official of Louis XI for his residence. Great trees towered protectingly above the Gothic turrets and balconies.

"Are you satisfied with your new home?" asked King Francis.

Leonardo held up a warning hand. "Hush, your majesty," he

pleaded. "Unless I am much mistaken I hear the sound of nesting doves."

"Yes, I see a dovecot yonder among the trees," cried Melzi.

"I know I shall be very happy here," Leonardo da Vinci told the king.

Chapter 23

FOR a few days the young nobleman and the two old servants unpacked the books and writing materials and household goods they had brought from Italy. Mathurine triumphantly hung her precious stewpot above the blackened bricks of the huge fireplace. Melzi untied the bundled notebooks and arranged them in neat piles in the carved chests at one end of the long chamber the master had chosen for his bedroom. On the walls he hung the pictures Leonardo had bade him bring from Rome: "Mona Lisa," the "Madonna with Saint Anne," and an unfinished study of a youth, effeminately beautiful.

Before they left Italy Francesco Melzi had ventured to question the master: "This young man sitting among the rocks? I have heard some of your pupils call him Bacchus; but others contend he is Saint John the Baptist. Which is he?"

"That you must decide for yourself," answered Leonardo da Vinci. The smile that hovered for a moment about his mouth seemed to Francesco to reflect the pictured smiles of Mona Lisa, of Saint Anne—yes, and the smile of this strange youth, who might well be either Christian saint or pagan god.

On Francis' first visit to Leonardo in his new home, the king's lively glance flitted from one picture to another; his eyes rested last and longest on the portrait of Mona Lisa.

"Who is she?" asked the king when at last he turned to the artist.

"The wife of a citizen of Florence, Francesco del Giocondo."

"How does it happen he allowed you to carry his wife's picture off to France?" demanded the visitor. Then as the old man flushed painfully and seemed to search for an answer, Francis' knightly tact prompted him to change the subject. He asked whether Leonardo had fully recovered from the fatigue of his journey; did he require any furnishings to make the château more comfortable? The steward at Amboise had heard that Leonardo seldom ate meat and begged to be allowed to furnish his table with fruits and vegetables from the royal gardens.

When the king was ready to depart, he turned again to the pictured face of Mona Lisa and studied it long and seriously. At last he asked: "Is this portrait for sale—and at what price?"

Again Leonardo da Vinci flushed painfully; but now he was ready with his reply. "I cannot sell it, your majesty." His tone was respectful but determined.

"It should be worth, say, four thousand gold crowns to me," suggested King Francis.

Francesco Melzi, who at the king's entrance had bowed and withdrawn to a respectful distance at one end of the long bedchamber, gasped at the sum. But Leonardo appeared unmoved.

"All that I have belongs to your majesty," he said. "When I am dead the portrait is yours, a small return for your many gracious kindnesses. But I must beg you to allow me to keep it while I live. It is the only possession I really value."

King Francis smiled his wide, boyish smile. "I thought the payment I offered large enough to tempt a poor man," he said.

"But I am not a poor man," Leonardo protested. "I have always believed that only the man who desires many things is poor. And I am rich in contentment."

"And you are also selfish," accused the king. "You would keep for your own pleasure what should bring delight to many. That picture, which fascinates me more than any I have ever seen, should belong to the world!"

"I have promised that it shall belong to you after my death," Leonardo assured him. "If you wish me to set it down in my will . . ."

"Agreed! And you shall receive the promised payment well in advance, I trust. Speaking of wills . . . You have heard, of course, how Pope Alexander VI, after the great discoveries, drew a line down the middle of the Atlantic Ocean on the new map and gave half of the world to Spain and half to Portugal?" Leonardo nodded. "Now, since you are a learned man, maybe you can tell me whether Adam left a will and named the Holy Father as executor."

The king's laughter suggested that he appreciated his own wit. Suddenly he grew sober. "I am glad of your promise," he told Leonardo. "I shall hang your wonderful painting in my palace at Fontainebleau. Perhaps, who knows, if I build an addition to the old Louvre and a room or two is set aside for a gallery—but that is far in the future."

"Yes, far in the future," echoed Leonardo politely.

King Francis in spite of his enthusiasm for Leonardo's paintings welcomed him to France more heartily as architect and engineer.

At the suggestion of Louise of Savoy Leonardo designed a castle and garden at Romorantin for the king's mother. Unfortunately Francis I, like Duke Ludovico, conceived an idea one day only to forget it on the morrow. The castle was never built, the garden never planted. But several of Leonardo da Vinci's ideas were probably utilized in the imposing castle of Chambord.

Francis spoke also of reconstructing his summer home at Amboise. The king did not need his new architect to point out to him that the castle was a sad jumble of various schools of architecture and could not compare either in beauty or comfort with the palaces Francis had seen in Italy. He listened attentively to Leonardo's plans: huge halls for the masques and balls that the king loved so dearly; such details as lavatories, which would be truly sanitary in an age without sanitation; fire prevention.

But Francis I was so busy urging a French architect to finish his new castle at Blois that he soon lost interest in improving the palace where he had spent his boyhood. Leonardo, with a shrug which had grown more patient with the passing years, put the plans away together with his ideas for fabricated houses. Leonardo had told the king of his plan to construct moveable huts. The parts might be built in the nearest town from which they could easily be carried to that spot in the forest where King Francis intended to set up his temporary court. The small but weatherproof dwellings could be erected at a day's notice. And, if the king pleased, Leonardo added, when the royal hunting party departed the little houses could be carried piecemeal back to town to furnish shelter to the homeless of the local population. Francis had liked the suggestion. He knew that when he and a large group of courtiers traveled to some distant and primitive hunting lodge it was often difficult to find decent sleeping quarters for the entire company.

But a far more ambitious scheme now appealed to Francis I. The king gladly granted permission to his royal engineer to make a detailed study of the courses of the Loire, the Sauldre, and other rivers. Leonardo seemed to renew his youth; as in the days when he had served Duke Ludovico and Cesare Borgia and the city-state of Florence, he felt himself not only the planner but the doer. Again he suggested canals and dams; again he drew exquisite maps and diagrams; he added the minutest details of harnessing torrential waters to drive mills, of diverting a certain amount for fountains.

Although Leonardo da Vinci's plan of a waterway to connect the many royal palaces met with the king's approval, Francis became involved in a matter he considered much more important.

He was the father of two daughters; but a girl-child did little to reassure King Francis in his hope that some day his heir would sit upon the French throne. Now a boy, beautiful and sturdy, was born to banish his father's fears. When the dauphin was baptized, Pope Leo himself consented to act as godfather.

The pope sent his nephew to act as his proxy. Lorenzo de' Medici was handsome and dashing, the hope of his ambitious family. In compliment to the king it was said that young Lorenzo journeyed from Italy to grace the dauphin's christening. But Francis I knew better. He himself had been seeking for a suitable French wife for Lorenzo. So now in the spring of 1518, Lorenzo de' Medici had come to Amboise to carry the papal blessing to the little dauphin and to claim his bride, whose delicate hands, it was hoped, would bind France and Italy in even closer friendship.

Leonardo watched Madeleine de la Tour d'Auvergne as, weighed down by her heavy brocade and her proud name, she moved slowly, almost timidly, through the month-long celebration of her marriage and the royal christening.

She was so young! thought Leonardo. He pitied her with the pity the old and sad must feel for those who stand untried and unaware of sorrow on the threshold of life. The music and the singing and the dancing, the young laughter of Madeleine's attendants and their handsome gallants, reminded the gray-haired man of his own lost youth in far-off Florence. He remembered, too, the songs another Lorenzo, the bridegroom's grandfather, had written for the merrymakers on a bright May morning long ago.

Never, agreed the guests, had there been such regal entertainment. The fountains in the gardens around Amboise gushed wine; beeves, roasted whole, dripped succulent juices on the flaming logs beneath the spits and filled the nostrils of the diners with teasing odors. Even more than the banqueting, the wedding guests enjoyed the tournament that continued for seven days in the great square before the castle. King Francis, laughing with excitement, still as agile as a boy in his teens, won victory after victory in the mimic battles he loved so well.

At the end of the jousting the French courtiers and Lorenzo de' Medici's huge retinue were astounded by the work of the king's engineer—or was it a wizard? For overnight there appeared in the square before the castle what seemed a great rampart crowned with many towers.

This scenery stretched across the castle moat. Between the more distant towers the spectators spied guns, which suddenly fired across the square while huge balls burst from the "enemy's" cannons. Again there was a mimic battle with the forces of Amboise, generaled by the king himself, and the army which poured from the "fortress" led by the duke of Alençon. The ladies especially enjoyed the spectacle since none of them had ever been privileged to witness an actual battle. They were thrilled at the bloodshed when some of those who fought on foot were wounded and when in the skirmishing many of the actors fell to rise no more.

They enjoy this as much as yesterday's spectacle, when a lion from the royal zoo was forced to defend itself against three wild and hungry dogs, thought Leonardo bitterly. Even the king's sister, although she is a true poet and has the face of a saint, has not covered her eyes. . . . He had not foreseen bloody deaths in this foolish game he had devised so long after his plans for making warfare more effective.

King Francis left the battlefield with its painted background and slippery crimson pavement and hurried to his bedchamber to remove his heavy armor. As he wiped his sweaty face, he ordered his attendants to prepare a hot bath. The gentlemen who left to heat the water exchanged glances of disrespectful amusement.

There was truth and to spare in the gossip, they thought, that since the young king had returned from Italy he was as fastidious as certain great ladies of the court. These damsels were said to take so many baths that they actually risked their health. Now their heroic king, who still suffered from some of the overrefinements he had picked up from effeminate princes in Italy, instead of pouring perfume over his sweaty body demanded hot water. The gentlemen of the royal bedchamber shook their heads over such modern degeneracy.

While Francis bathed, Leonardo listened to his pleased comments on the day's performance. "You have done very well, my Leonardo. But tomorrow—ah, tomorrow—should be the climax of our month's revelries. But how will you be able to surpass what has gone before?"

"My masque has been well rehearsed," Leonardo assured Francis as the king reached for one of the tall pitchers and poured yet another torrent over his broad shoulders.

"But the scenery for today's fortifications is not yet cleared away. You have not had time to arrange the background on which I know you have labored so untiringly," puzzled King Francis.

"That there might be time to arrange all in perfect order, I decided to stage my 'Paradiso' in the courtyard before the château you have so graciously lent me," answered Leonardo da Vinci. "It will be a pleasant short walk for your guests. When they arrive at Cloux tomorrow evening all will be in readiness, for my actors know their cues and my musicians are well-trained." He sighed a little. "No one remembers it, but I was once an admired lute-player."

"But from what you told me," persisted Francis, "the shifting of the scenery is most complicated. I think you said you planned to have a revolving stage, whatever that is."

"Something that I invented many years ago in Italy. And though my audience will marvel at what I shall show them, there is nothing complicated in the tasks I have assigned tomorrow night's workers. It is just a matter of levers and pulleys."

But the delighted guests the next evening decided Leonardo's masque was more a matter of witchcraft. Again, as in Milan, stars appeared in a sky of shining blue; the planets moved in harmony. Lovely music brought new beauty to the summer night. Having grown old, Leonardo was more easily moved than in his reserved youth. But he was ashamed of his tears and withdrew into the shadows to hide them; only Melzi saw the master weep over the beauty he had twice created and which would in a few hours again fade into nothingness.

The devoted friend and disciple could not know that Leonardo wept also when he looked on the frail beauty of the bride seated in her gilded chair between King Francis and Lorenzo de' Medici. The old man remembered another bride, who had watched his "Paradiso" unfold, a child who did not dream of the years of dark disappointment and humiliation that would follow her loveless wedding.

Leonardo had just heard that among the many splendid presents Pope Leo had sent tonight's bride was a marriage bed of tortoise shell decorated with pearls and emeralds. Now there suddenly came to the aged Florentine the memory of Simonetta stretched upon another bed—no, not a marriage but a funeral bed, and it had been decorated not with jewels but with the jewel-bright flowers of spring.

He shuddered for this girl's future—although he knew not why. Because the heavy years had taught him that death is often far more merciful than life, he might have pitied her less had he known that within a year she, too, would be carried to rest in a tomb in Florence. Nor could he dream of the fate of the baby girl, left fatherless and motherless and unprotected. Many years later she was known and feared as Catherine de' Medici, Queen of France.

All that rested in the future as black as the velvet beret Leonardo doffed when he bent before King Francis I.

"You have indeed done well," King Francis assured his court painter. His merry eyes darkened with concern as they noted the old man's deadly pallor and shaking hands. "The master is not well," Francis told Melzi. "Help him to his bed. Tomorrow I will send my own physician to attend him."

It had been a long, weary day and Leonardo da Vinci was glad to rest. He knew he should try to sleep but for the first time in his life he abhorred the idea of remaining alone; he was like a child who fears the darkness.

Ashamed of his secret fears and torments, Leonardo at last called Francesco Melzi to his bedside.

"Yes, master?" said Melzi and waited for him to speak.

There were so many matters Leonardo longed to speak of, for tonight's repetition of his masque had stirred up many memories. But he did not know how to begin. And would Francesco understand? Suddenly Leonardo realized how high a wall of silence can arise even between two who love each other dearly. Again he thought of that festal night in Milan and the untroubled young eyes of Duchess Isabella.

"It was so long ago!" he murmured.

Although Francesco Melzi had leaned over the bed to catch every word, he did not understand.

Chapter 24

$\mathcal{T}$HE bed on which Leonardo now spent many hours was richly canopied with crimson velvet; the deep chairs which stood before the huge brick fireplace were covered with the same material, the arms of the house of Valois worked upon their high backs in golden thread. King Francis had sent them from his own apartments at Amboise. On days when the sick man felt strong enough to rise for a little space, he liked to sit very close to the fire, for in the cold and damp of the winter of 1518 not even his heavy black cloak, lined with fur, kept him warm.

Whenever Francis I visited Leonardo and found him huddled before the fireplace, the king occupied the second chair. They would sit together like master and pupil, Leonardo still eager to teach, Francis eager to learn from one he esteemed so highly. But even such quiet talks tired the aged philosopher. He bade Melzi bar the door to other visitors.

Leonardo continued to shield himself from interruptions even when the first warmth of an early spring restored something of his former vigor. For he knew how little time remained for the many things which he still planned to do.

Since coming to France Leonardo had made spasmodic efforts to classify and rearrange his chaotic notebooks. Now with unlimited leisure and Melzi's intelligent aid, the results of a lifetime of study and investigation might be prepared for publication; at least the works on painting and on anatomy! But what of his study on the human voice, on optics? No, it would be better to revise his conclusions on hydrodynamics. Or, perhaps, he should return to his old love, geology.

"The trouble, master," commented Melzi, when Leonardo first discussed his perplexities with his friend, "is that you have set down more than a dozen other men could possibly record in a busy lifetime."

"Yet I have finished so little!" Leonardo pushed a page toward his friend and pointed out each item as he read. "See how I planned to write fifteen books on water. The first on water in itself. The second concerning the sea. Then springs and rivers. The ninth book would discuss the things that dwell in it. The thirteenth would treat machines turned by water. And . . ."

"Mercy, master!" Melzi cried in burlesqued terror. "The mere outline sets my poor head spinning like a whirlpool."

"Then this outline would please you better since you are far more familiar with the arts than the sciences." Holding the paper closer, as his eyes now often clouded, Leonardo read a list of subjects to be developed which he had long ago jotted down: Perspective. Artists' Materials. Casting. Sculpture. Music.

Suddenly the younger man chuckled with amusement.

"Here," said Melzi, "is a page on which you made mathematical diagrams and sketched architectural plans. All as beautifully done as your drawings for Pacioli's book, which I once heard someone compare to the lovely decorations in a rare 'Book of Hours.' On the same page are notes on acoustics and an anatomical specimen. Yet in the lower right-hand corner you have written—in legible script for once . . ." Again he chuckled.

"And what is so amusing about my note in the lower right-hand corner?" Leonardo asked a little sharply.

"I am sure you judged yourself too harshly," answered Francesco

Melzi. "On that page, which shows something of your labors in four fields of research, you inscribed: 'I have wasted my hours.'"

Now he laughed outright; but Leonardo da Vinci did not seem amused. "Somewhere in these jumbled pages," he said soberly, "I set down certain axioms for a certain Leonardo da Vinci to follow. And one ran: 'Shun those studies in which the work that results dies with the worker.' You praise me for my labors in many fields. But, Francesco, if I had been content to till a tiny plot—to wait in patience for the harvest . . . Michelangelo, Raphael—they will never be haunted by unfinished pictures like those that come to plague me in my sleepless midnight hours."

Francesco Melzi, who had often silently grieved to see his master neglect his painting, could think of no reply. He saw that the old man had slipped into a mood of dark depression and tried to divert him.

"Master, Mathurine tells me that when she went out to gather twigs for this morning's breakfast pot, she heard a lark sing. But is it not too early in the year to hear the lark?"

Leonardo smiled. "Now perhaps you will be convinced that I have indeed wasted my time. Think how many useless facts I have recorded in these books. Consider my Bestiary with stories of the toad and the ermine and bits picked up here and there about my little friends, the birds. When you spoke of the lark just now I remembered that I had set down the old superstition which so many of our countrymen believe."

"I know no superstition about the lark," confessed Melzi.

"Perhaps your peasant nurse warned you but you have forgotten," answered Leonardo. "I am sure she told you never to bring a lark into the presence of one who is ill. For if the sick person is going to die, the bird turns away its head and refuses to look at him. So bid Mathurine," and he tried to speak lightly, "never to bring the bird into my sick chamber."

"But if the patient will recover?" questioned Francesco.

"I have it all set down. The bird never takes his eyes off him and is the cause, it is said, of all sickness leaving him."

"I wonder that you who have recorded so many observations

about birds should heed such nonsense," commented Melzi, who prided himself that as a modern he had no use for ancient superstitions. He turned another page; hesitated; spoke diffidently. "Here is a picture of a great bird—no, it is a bat. Not a real bat but the sketched model of a machine with wings. Salai once told me in Milan . . ."

"Salai in his manhood is an even greater liar than when he was a boy, since he has lived more years to invent his falsehoods," said Leonardo gruffly.

"I did not mean to pry," stammered Melzi. "But many have asked me whether it ever rose from the earth?"

"To such pryers and peepers," Leonardo told him, "you can answer in perfect truth that you know nothing." He turned his eyes to the portrait of Mona Lisa. Francesco Melzi saw with startled wonder that the woman's smile, which seemed to say everything yet said nothing, was mirrored in the master's face. Yet how could he be certain since the evening twilight which crept through the narrow windows had already begun to fill the room with shadows?

The next afternoon when the two sat again looking over the notebooks several visitors came to Cloux. Leonardo did not refuse to see them. The king had been absent from Amboise for the past few weeks; the old man missed his chatter and wished that others from the outside world might come to break the monotony which had begun to weigh heavily upon him.

Leonardo bade Melzi bring him a mirror and he carefully combed his long white hair and flowing beard. With his usual fastidiousness he examined his nails and made sure that his long black cloak was free of dust. Then he forced back his tired shoulders and sat proudly erect, a prince of painters prepared to welcome a prince of the church.

When Luis, the Cardinal of Aragon, entered with his secretary, Antonio de Beatis, the feeble old man tried to rise. But the cardinal waved him back to his chair and seated himself near the fireplace. As the two talked, Francesco hastily picked up the loose sheets which had fallen from Leonardo's lap and lay scattered upon the floor. The secretary offered to assist; together the two men carried the heavy books back to the chests that stood at the further end of the room.

Antonio gasped when he caught a glimpse of the closely packed volumes in the chest Melzi had opened to receive the notebooks he carried. Francesco pointed to the chests that stood in a long row.

"They are also full," he said not without pride.

"I heard in Rome that he had filled an infinite number of volumes with his scientific observations," answered the young secretary, "but I could not believe it. Will they be published?"

Francesco Melzi glanced toward the fireplace where his master and the cardinal seemed too deeply engrossed to hear anything that might be said at the other end of the long room. Still he lowered his voice.

"I fear it is impossible. It would be a task for Hercules to rearrange and classify the material the master has taken a lifetime to gather but has never found leisure to revise. If he were still well and strong . . ." He shrugged hopelessly.

"I am sure his works would prove most profitable if they could be enjoyed by scholars and scientists," said the secretary. "I am neither and my judgment must be of little worth. But certain humanists have told me that Leonardo da Vinci is a man of the rarest achievements."

"Nor do I lay claim to scholarship," answered Francesco Melzi with equal modesty. "But the master has permitted me to examine these books he has compiled through the years; he has talked to me of many things. And from what I have seen and heard I am willing to affirm that Leonardo da Vinci is the greatest intellect of our time."

"Nay," Antonio de Beatis contradicted him. "Do not say the greatest intellect of our time. Say rather 'of *all* times.' For not one man among the Greeks or Romans could do so many things and do them all so well."

After the cardinal and his secretary had departed, Melzi lost no time in repeating Antonio's tribute.

"Master," he declared, "the young man is right. He confesses that he is no scholar; but he has traveled much and because of his connections has met many learned men. And he insists that these notebooks must be published."

"There is no time," answered Leonardo, a little painfully. "Time, the great destroyer, will destroy me and my work together. Because of my youthful idleness, which I have so often regretted, I know little Latin. But the poetry I read in that tongue brought me much happiness and now snatches come back to me like remembered music. I was thinking only this morning of something I read in Horace; or was it Ovid? It was so long ago that I last read the lovely verses. They describe Helen, fairest of women, in her old age. Do you remember them, my son?"

Francesco Melzi nodded; his heart burned with pity for the broken man before him. His eyes tried to avoid Leonardo's shriveled, helpless hands, the hands that had covered page after page in the notebooks with profound deductions and matchless illustrations; the hands that painted Mona Lisa, now smiling down from the opposite wall.

At last Leonardo continued, speaking as though to himself, in the manner of the aged:

"She looked into her mirror and saw the wrinkles which Time had scrawled upon her face. Then she wept and wondered why twice a man had been so ensnared by her beauty that he had carried her away from home and country. For Time had destroyed that beauty which destroyed Troy."

The quavering voice sank to a whisper:

"O Time, great devourer, and you, envious Age, together you destroy all things, beauty of woman and the mind of man. And slowly gnawing with your teeth you finally consume all things in lingering death."

Chapter 25

SEVERAL days later the sixty-seven-year-old Florentine sent for Guillaume Boureau, who served as notary to the king at Amboise. The late April sunlight streamed warmly through the narrow windows of the château at Cloux, but Leonardo huddled in the folds of his heavy fur-lined cloak and a fire burned in the huge brick fireplace for his comfort.

The notary, a brisk, obsequious little man in his middle years, bowed low to the court painter. "Ah," burbled the lawyer, bound to be agreeable although he sacrificed truth to his kind intentions, "ah, how well you look this bright spring morning."

Leonardo surveyed his visitor from beneath his shaggy white eyebrows. "The soul parts from the body with extreme reluctance," he quoted sourly. This nervous little man with the forced smile who stood before him rubbing his hands together vaguely irritated Leonardo. "I look as I feel and I feel far from well 'this bright spring morning.' If I were not on the threshold of death I would not have sent for you. Now, please sit there and take down my last will and testament."

Leonardo had always despised the trickery of the law and the smooth dealings of lawyers. Yet his father, the notary, would have approved of the legal exactness with which his impractical son disposed of his not inconsiderable possessions. He even remembered to give Francesco Melzi his proper title, and carefully designated the dear companion of his last years as a "nobleman of Milan."

Leonardo's half-brothers had tried to bring shame and grief upon him as their father's illegitimate son, that they might deprive him of his share of the family inheritance. But now Leonardo da Vinci with a touch of unusual irony called them his "brothers-in-blood in Florence" and designated for them the four hundred ducats still deposited to his credit in that city. To them he also bequeathed a certain property at Fiesole.

To Mathurine, the faithful old woman who had followed him to France, Leonardo left the cloak he now wore and a matching cap as well as two ducats. Her fellow servant, Battista, was to receive one-half of Leonardo's vineyard near Milan.

Salai had never shown himself either a dutiful adopted son or a faithful friend. But Leonardo could not forget how he had once loved the handsome youth. He now dictated that Salai was to receive the other half of the Milanese property where he had dwelt for some time with his family.

The old man's voice faltered, for he had grown very tired. He forced himself to continue his dictation. He felt that he could never sufficiently repay Francesco Melzi for "his kindness in the past." Leonardo knew that his disciple's modest wants would always be safely covered by the inheritance from his father. But in payment for Melzi's services as executor he was to receive all the money in Leonardo's possession at his death as well as any salary still due him from the king.

But what would gold mean to one who had long served so faithfully and pure-heartedly and without thought of gain? Leonardo realized that Francesco Melzi was as sentimental as any woman. He would treasure anything that had once belonged to his loved master. So Leonardo bequeathed to him all of his clothing except the "cloak of good black cloth lined with fur."

Then came the legacy which the master knew would please

Francesco most: "Each and all of the books which the said testator has at present, and other instruments and portraits connected with his art and occupation of painter."

Leonardo leaned back in his chair and smiled. This fussy little man, busily inscribing the last bequest on the long parchment, like all the world considered him only as a painter. To the notary "books" would mean nothing but the few scattered about Leonardo's chamber, printed reference works, and several handwritten manuscripts which were already becoming somewhat rare and were therefore valuable. But Melzi had spent many hours of late turning the pages of the notebooks. He would know how to treasure such a legacy.

Leonardo smiled but without malice when the witnesses whom the notary had chosen entered the room. They were the vicar of the church of Saint Denis at Amboise, two of his priests and two Franciscans. Once I might have shocked these God-fearing men with my godless opinions, thought the dying philosopher. But now above all things I long for peace.

He yearned not only for peace but the sense of belonging. From his boyhood days he had been a wanderer, without a family and a home, without allegiance to any city that had sheltered him or to any ruler who had proved a friend. He had never defied the Church openly and had served her with his art. Yet had he not earned the accusation that he preferred to be a philosopher rather than a Christian?

It suddenly flashed through Leonardo's mind that he had long been both. I have been a philosopher, a lover of wisdom, he thought. But I have also tried to be a Christian, who always carried God in his heart and tried in his own poor way to follow in the footsteps of His Son.

"And your funeral?" asked Melzi, speaking through his tears. "Tell us your wishes now and I shall see that everything shall be as you have said."

Leonardo knew of Melzi's faith, the faith of a simple child. It would comfort him a little in his grief if his beloved master were granted all the last customary honors. But that means that before

my death I must receive the Holy Sacraments, Leonardo thought with a sudden renewal of his old rapier-sharp keenness. And why not? I have never been a zealous son of the Church; but I have never rebelled against my Mother. After all my wanderings, I will turn to her and she will bring me home.

Leonardo da Vinci watched the joy kindle in Melzi's wet eyes as he requested the last rites of the Church. He then arranged in every detail for a funeral which would be in accord with his life as he had tried to live it—dignified, in good taste, without ostentation. No monument, he hastily decided. Let his works be his true memorial. He went on to designate the three churches in which masses were to be recited; how many candles should be burned; how many torches carried in his funeral procession. He wished, he said, to be buried in the chapel of Amboise, if the king graciously approved. And he added that all present should pray that King Francis might return from Saint Germain in time to bid his grateful servant farewell.

Leonardo left his bed again only to take the Holy Sacrament. Leaning upon Melzi's arm he compelled his shaking legs to support him. Leonardo knew the ways of courts and desired to meet his King in seemly fashion. He wished that the earthly king who had treated him with such gracious affection in the sunset years would return to Cloux for a last visit. He strained his failing ears to catch a familiar footstep at the threshold.

Even before the priest with his young acolytes left the death chamber, Melzi and Battista had helped Leonardo to his alcoved bed. Mathurine hastened to arrange his pillows. He thanked her with his gentle, yet half-mocking smile and it was to her he roused himself to speak.

"Mathurine, the youngest acolyte—the boy with golden hair like a nimbus about his head . . . ?"

The old woman nodded.

"He is the eldest child of a gentleman of the court." Mathurine, who was a born gossip, forgot her grief for a moment in her eagerness to babble everything she had picked up in the kitchen at Amboise. "A clever lad! Once I heard the chief cook say . . ."

She rambled on and on, although Leonardo no longer seemed to listen.

The youngest acolyte had held a lighted candle, a candle which rayed forth light like the sun at midsummer. The feast of Saint John. Florence. The sun. It turned Giotto's doors to gold. I was always drawn to the picture of Daedalus. He aimed to fly to the sun but he fell, fell. . . . For Saint John . . . dancing . . . splendid horses. My colossus. Springtime. Lorenzo. Florence. Always spring. . . .

Battista wiped his eyes; then took the arm of the weeping woman and led her toward the door. He whispered that for a little while they should leave Francesco Melzi alone with his dead.

*   *   *   *

The purple pageantry of death drew slowly to a close. The memorial candles flickered low in their sockets; the brightness of the sixty torches, which chosen pensioners of the parish almshouse carried in the funeral procession, was quenched. But not forever! Leonardo da Vinci in planning his burial remembered how short the distance was from the château of Cloux to the royal chapel at Amboise. He had calculated how long the torches would burn and had thriftily suggested that they should afterwards be distributed among the neighborhood churches that they might be used again.

In the courtyard of the château of Cloux old Mathurine rolled back her sleeves and pinned up her skirts before she began to scour the threshold. It had seemed strange that morning not to prepare the sick man's frugal breakfast; she missed his welcoming smile from the canopied bed in the room she had just scrubbed and aired.

But a woman with a house to clean and two men left to cook for has no time to mourn, she told herself severely. Such a luxury was only for fine folks of the court who had often come to visit the master in his studio; she doubted not that even King Francis would grieve when he heard of Leonardo's passing. He will soon forget, decided Mathurine, for kings forget easily. But I will never forget.

I would remember him all my days for his gentle courtesy, even if he had not left me his very own black coat lined with fur—and two whole ducats.

A sturdy, black-eyed boy of four dashed through the door of the gardener's cottage and ran to her across the cobblestones. Mathurine, who had lost her husband and her baby years before, had learned to love the child whom she liked to consider as her own grandson. Now when he gave her his morning kiss, she hugged him close to her withered breasts.

He wriggled himself loose. "See what I caught, granny," he shrilled. Opening his hand he showed her a crushed and torn white butterfly. His lips quivered. "Master Leonardo told me not to hurt . . ."

"You must have squeezed it too hard. Throw it away, now it's dead," advised Mathurine.

"What's *dead*?" asked the child as he stared at the broken wings. "When I asked mother yesterday to let me go up to visit Master Leonardo, she said he was dead. And I'd never see him any more. Where is he? Where did he go?"

In the room where Leonardo da Vinci had worked and pondered and died, Francesco Melzi rested from his task of packing his treasures for carriage back to Milan. Notebook after notebook, each filled to overflowing with drawings and notations; this was not the time to count the manuscript pages but Melzi computed they would number from five to six thousand. He would take the precious sketches and writings to his father's old house near Milan and devote the rest of his life to preparing them for publication.

His dream like the dreams of the master was never to be realized. Although Melzi's devotion never wavered through all the fifty years which remained to him, he was unable to complete the task his love and admiration had set.

"Who but a Leonardo," he used to say, as his eyes grew dim with age, "can edit a Leonardo!"

At Francesco Melzi's death the long-treasured manuscripts were scattered and fell into the hands of many owners in many lands. Some were lost but over five thousand precious pages survived. A miracle, Melzi in his simple faith would have proclaimed their survival. But Leonardo da Vinci, sceptical of miracles since he had always believed there could be no result without a cause, would have been sadly puzzled.

Now, as he packed the sketches and books, Melzi looked out through the half-open casement upon the trees that were gently leafing under the warm sun of early May. How the master had always loved the spring! For him there had been a new world to explore in every tree and flower. In the swallows which after their winter's journey had haunted the windowsill expectant of crumbs, he seemed to have found an eternal challenge.

What was this mystery of flight that Leonardo da Vinci had studied so long and passionately? Melzi smiled sadly as he again scanned the top sheet of the notebook on the table before him. Yes, here it stood written:

The swallow has its wings quite different from those of the kite, for it is very narrow in the shoulder, and long in the span of the wing. Its stroke when it flies is made up of two distinct actions, that is, the span of the wing is spread out like an oar in the direction of the tail, the shoulder toward the earth. . . .

Francesco remembered Leonardo's strange and daring prophecy: "The Great Bird will take its first flight . . ." How often he had longed to ask the master of the mysterious flight which was to fill the world with "amazement." Once, he had ventured to question Leonardo. . . . And now he would never know.

Where is he now? Melzi mused, as perplexed as the little boy who played beneath the half-open windows. What new flight does his spirit dare through the darkness? They buried his worn body in the royal chapel. I will surely go there to weep above his grave before I return to Italy. But his mind, as restless as a wild bird, will never be weighted down beneath the earth. Long after I am turned to dust, wise men will read these writings and honor him for what he has set down so bravely. And perhaps the wisest and boldest of them all will carry to triumph the dreams Leonardo dreamed in his loneliness.

Melzi forced himself to break off his musings that he might return to his task. He had already distributed many of the master's benefactions; carried out his slightest wish for the order of his funeral. As soon as all necessary preparations for the homeward journey were completed, he would write to the da Vinci brothers, who were undeserving. Franceso thought bitterly, of either Leonardo's legacy or his forgiveness. Would they grieve even for a moment, as Francesco felt he must sorrow for the rest of his years?

At Saint Germain King Francis had waited beside Queen Claude for the birth of their fourth child. On his return to Amboise, his joy in welcoming a second son clouded when he learned of the passing of his admired painter. Kings might be fickle in their friendship, according to old Mathurine. But when Melzi described Leonardo's last days the light-hearted monarch wept openly and unashamed.

King Francis carried away from Cloux the precious portrait of Mona Lisa. In the pictured smile he believed he saw reflected the very smile of Leonardo da Vinci. The king looked long and earnestly at the lips which seemed to ask a question they would never answer.

That night as Francesco Melzi bent over the master's desk, he also thought of the smile brooding on the pictured face that he would never see again. If only the king had allowed his purchase to remain on the wall of Leonardo's bedchamber just a few weeks longer! Francesco sighed as he began his letter to the da Vinci family:

To me he was like the best of fathers [he wrote painfully], for whose death it would be impossible for me to express the grief I have felt; and so long as these my limbs endure I shall possess a perpetual sorrow, and with good reason, since he showed to me day by day the warmest love and devotion. But everyone, I think, should mourn the loss of such a man, whose like nature cannot again produce.

Bibliography

Benetix, Fernando. *In the Footsteps of Cortez*. New York: Pantheon Books, 1952.

Bowra, Sir Maurice (comp.). *Golden Ages of the Great Cities*. London, New York: Thames and Hudson, 1952.

Brion, Marcel. *Michelangelo*. New York: The Greystone Press, 1940.

Camp, L. Sprague de and Ley, Willy. *Lands Beyond*. New York: Rinehart and Company, Inc., 1952.

Clark, Kenneth. *Leonardo da Vinci*. Cambridge: Cambridge University Press, 1939.

Cottler, Joseph. *Man with Wings*. Boston: Little, Brown and Company, 1942.

Dampier, Sir William Cecil D. *A History of Science*. New York: The Macmillan Co., 1949.

Dibner, Bern. *Leonardo da Vinci, Military Engineer*. New York: Burndy Library, Inc., 1946.

Freud, Sigmund. *Leonardo da Vinci, a Psychosexual Study of an Infantile Reminiscence*. New York: Moffat, Yard & Co., 1916.

Goldscheider, Ludwig. *Leonardo da Vinci*. New York: Oxford University Press, 1948.

Leonardo da Vinci: Landscapes and Plants. New York: Garden City Books—Phaidon Publishers, 1952.

Gombrich, E. H. *The Story of Art*. New York: Phaidon Publishers, Inc., 1950.

Hackett, Francis. *Francis the First*. New York: Doubleday, Doran & Co., 1935.

Merejkowski, Dmitri. *The Romance of Leonardo da Vinci.* New York: The Modern Library, 1928.

Morison, Samuel Eliot. *Admiral of the Ocean Sea.* Boston: Little, Brown and Company, 1942.

Myers, Bernard. *Fifty Great Artists.* New York: Bantam Books, 1953.

O'Malley, Charles D. and Saunders, J. B. de C. M. *Leonardo da Vinci on the Human Body.* New York: Henry Schuman, 1952.

Ripley, Elizabeth. *Leonardo da Vinci.* New York: Oxford University Press, 1952.

Roeder, Ralph. *The Man of the Renaissance.* New York: The Viking Press, 1933.

Saponaro, Michele. *Michelangelo Buonarroti.* New York: Pellegrini and Cudahy, 1950.

Singer, C. J. *From Magic to Science.* New York: Boni and Liveright, 1928.

Sirén, Osvald. *Leonardo da Vinci, the Artist and the Man.* New Haven: Yale University Press, 1916.

Stearns, Frank Preston. *The Midsummer of Italian Art.* New York: G. P. Putnam's Sons, 1895.

Symonds, John Addington. *Life of Michelangelo.* New York: Charles Scribner, 1925.

Renaissance in Italy—The Fine Arts. New York: Smith, Elder and Company, 1903.

Taylor, Rachel Annand. *Leonardo the Florentine.* New York: Harper and Brothers, 1928.

Vallentin, Antonina. *Leonardo da Vinci.* New York: The Viking Press, 1938.

Vasari, Giorgio. *The Life of Leonardo da Vinci.* New York: Longmans, Green & Co., 1903.

Vinci, Leonardo da. *The Notebooks of Leonardo da Vinci.* New York: Reynal & Hitchcock, 1938.

Pamphlets and Periodicals

Heydenreich, Ludwig Heinrich. "Leonardo da Vinci the Scientist." New York: International Business Machines Corporation, 1951.

Sarton, George. "Leonardo da Vinci." New York: *Book of the Month Club,* Inc., 1952.

Storer, John H. "Bird Aerodynamics." New York: *Scientific American,* April, 1952.

Index

187

About the Author

ELMA EHRLICH LEVINGER was born in Chicago and attended schools there. After working her way through the University of Chicago, she attended Radcliffe on a year's fellowship studying drama. This led to the writing of plays, many of which won prizes in national contests. Mrs. Levinger has written short stories—she sold her first to *McCall's* when she was nineteen—textbooks, two adult novels and then turned to biography for young people. With her husband she did a considerable amount of traveling throughout the world, but they made their home in California.

A fascinating study of Leonardo da Vinci—master painter, sculptor and architect, scientist engineer and inventor.

In this amazing story of the most versatile genius who ever lived, Elma Levinger pays due respect to the painter, but she places particular emphasis on his discoveries in science and his inventions in mechanics and engineering that might well be the product of a twentieth-century mind, rather than those of a fifteenth-century Renaissance painter.

Leonardo evidenced unusual artistic talent when still very young, and his father sent him to Florence, apprenticing him to one of the leading artists of that city. Here da Vinci worked for ten years, perfecting the techniques of his craft and exploring the sciences of botany, zoology, biology and anatomy which he felt were closely related to art.

Through the good graces of Lorenzo the Magnificent, ruler of Florence, Leonardo was summoned to the Court of Milan. Here he spent his most productive years. Under the patronage of the Duke of Milan, the artist painted portraits and altar pieces, installed modern plumbing into the *castello* and filled his famous notebooks with designs of every type—from the Cathedral of Milan to the royal stables. During this period he worked out an elaborate scheme for ideal cities